AF559795

PLIGHT OF UNORGANISED WORKERS

PLIGHT OF UNORGANISED WORKERS

Edited by

Dr. A. SELVA KUMAR

M.Com., M.Phil., M.B.A., Ph.D.

Reader, Department of Commerce

Pope's College, Sawyerpuram

Thoothukudi District – 628 251

Tamil Nadu

(India)

DISCOVERY PUBLISHING HOUSE PVT. LTD.

NEW DELHI-110 002

First Published-2009

ISBN 978-81-8356-491-5

Published by:

DISCOVERY PUBLISHING HOUSE PVT. LTD.

4831/24, Ansari Road, Prahlad Street
Darya Ganj, New Delhi-110002 (India)
Phone: 23279245 • Fax: 91-11-23253475
E-mail: **dphbooks@rediffmail.com**
dphtemp@indiatimes.com
web: **www.discoverypublishinggroup.com**

Printed at:
Sachin Printers
Delhi

Foreword

Several studies pinpoint clearly the appalling working conditions of unorganized labour. Inadequate wages, casual nature of employment, hazardous jobs and so forth are the adversities met by the unorganized labour in the country.

Earlier, Dr. A. Selvakumar brought out a research book captioned "Child Labour in Home Based Sector" in the year 2005. Now Dr.A.Selvakumar as an editor has brought out another socially relevant book under the title "Plight of Unorganized Workers".

The book is rare of its kind in the arena of unorganized sector indicating varied problems of the workers in different businesses. The suggestions offered to tackle the major problems of the unorganized workers are found to be practical.

It is appreciable Dr. A. Selvakumar has taken strenuous effort in editing relevant articles pertaining to the unorganized sector. The articles correctly evaluate the problems of the unorganized labour.

I am quite sure that the book would enlighten the readers who are interested in unorganized sector. A warm appreciation is placed on record to Discovery Publishing House Pvt. Ltd., New Delhi for bringing out the book in time.

Dr. R. NEELAMEGAM
Emeritus Professor-AICTE
Department of Management Studies
V.H.N.S.N.College
Virudhunagar – 626 001,
Tamil Nadu

Preface

"My Grace is Sufficient for thee"
II Cor.12:9

At the outset, I praise Almighty God Jesus Christ for having showered His blessing on me to bring out this book. Without Him, this humble piece of work would not have been successfully published as book.

The concept of unorganized sector has been debated since it was first used in research done by the ILO in 1969. In ILO, employment categorization, the unorganized sectors include employers, employees, workers of micro enterprises, the self employed servants, occasional workers and non - remunerated family workers. Unorganised workers are relying on their own resources, operating in an unregulated and competitive market. The unorganized sector is said to shelter unemployed in general, the less privileged in society among them women, migrants, children, very young or very aged people who have no chance of finding a job in the formal sector the seemingly un employable. They are characterized by highly unexploitative, labour intensive discontinuous production, low productivity, use of unskilled labour etc. The problem of unorganized labour is very common.

Therefore, this book on,"Plight Of Unorganised Workers", aims to focus on the problems and prospects of unorganized labour in India. For this purpose, an attempt has been made by the author (Editor) to collect various articles/research papers related to workers working in various unorganised sectors.

This book is of immense use, as it throws light on various aspects on the problems of unorganised labour in our country.

Emirate scholar from various universities/colleges/institutions have contributed their research papers for publication. The efforts of all these contributors are highly appreciated/acknowledged. This book will be very helpful to policy makers, planners, teachers, research scholars, government, various non – government agencies, who are working for the development of the nation as a whole.

I sincerely hope that readers will find this book quite interesting and informative and will present a true picture of the situation, valuable suggestion and the feed back of all readers are always welcome.

After publishing my book on, "Child Labour in Home Based Sector", I got many appreciations and suggestions. Most of them were very encouraging and inspiring. This led me to edit more papers on," Plight of Unorganised Workers", of eminent authors of various universities/colleges/institutions and get them to publish in the form of a book. I am extremely thankful to all the authors who have contributed their research papers/articles in this book.

I express my gratitude to Dr.R.Neelamegam, Emeritus Professor – AICTE and Director, Institute of Management Studies, V.H.N.S.N. College, Virudhu Nagar, Tamilnadu, and formerly, Professor and Head, Department of Corporate Secretaryship, Alagappa University, Karaikudi, Tamilnadu, for having consented to write foreword for this book. His useful comments and suggestions encouraged me immensely to bring out this book.

My sincere thanks to Dr. G.Karunanithi, Professor and Head, Department of Sociology, Manonmaniam Sundaranar University, Tirunelveli, Tamilnadu for his kind encouragement and guidance to publish this book.

I sincerely thank, The Rt. Rev. Dr. J.A.D. Jebachandran, Chairman and Secretary, Pope's College, Sawyerpuram and Bishop of Thoothukudi- Nazareth Diocese, Tamilnadu, for his kind encouragement and prayer support to publish this book.

I heartily thank my friend Lt. D. Jeyasingh, Selection Grade Lecturer in Economics, Pope's College for his constant encouragement to publish this book.

I thank Mr. S.A.Senthil Kannan, CBI Officer, New Delhi, for his help to publish this book.

I thank Dr. T.Joseph Christadoss, Principal, Pope's College and my colleagues Mr. J.Arulraj Daniel, Head, Department of Commerce, Mrs. E.Sweety Stany, Head, Department of Business Administration, Mr. G.Koil Samuel, Lecturer, Mrs.J.Shobana□Joel, Lecturer, Mrs. D. Annie Selwyn, Lecturer, Mr.J.Johnson Asir, Lecturer, Mrs. J.Sheeba Jebasigh, Lecturer in Commerce and Mr. J. Jeyasingh, Selection Grade Lecturer in Economics, Pope's College, for interest shown by them to bring out this book.

I avail myself of this opportunity to express my deep sense of gratitude to my beloved parents, Mr. D.Ayyapillai and Mrs.A.Mariammal, my elder brother Dr. A.Arul Devadoss, in-laws Mr. N.Francis, Mrs. Leela Francis, Mr.F.Godwin and Mr. F.Suresh Jesuwin for all their moral and material support.

My dear wife Mrs.Graceline Julia Selvakumar, beloved daughters Selvi. S. Letishia Mary and Baby S.Ida Blessy were three silent and prayerful upholders to me to publish this book.

I, on behalf of all the contributors, friends and family members thank Mr.Tilak Wasan, Proprietor, Discovery Publishing House Pvt. Ltd., New Delhi for his kind help and co-operation on publishing this book.

Last but not least, I thank Mr. M.A. Mohamed Younoos, Proprietor, Master Computer Centre, Melapalayam, Tirunelveli, Tamil Nadu, for his help in computer typing work of this book.

A Selva Kumar

Contents

List of Contributors

1. **Dr. P. Anandharajakumar,** Lecturer in Rural Development (SS), Department of Rural Development, Gandhigram Rural University, Gandhigram.
2. **Mr. V. Duraisingh,** Lecturer in Economics, Manonmaniam Sundaranar University, Tirunelveli – 628 012, Tamil Nadu.
3. **Dr. Mrs R. Ezhil Jasmine,** Lecturer in Commerce, Government Arts College for Women, Sivagangai, Tamilnadu.
4. **Mr. C. Eugine Franco,** SG Lecturer in Commerce, St.Xaviers's College (Autonomous), Palayamkottai, Tamilnadu – 627 002.
5. **Dr. S. Gurusamy,** Professor and Head, Department of Sociology, Gandhigram Rural University, Gandhigram– 624 302, Dindigul, Tamilnadu.
6. **Dr. S. Kannan,** Reader in Commerce, Kamaraj College, Thoothukudi – 628 001, Tamilnadu.
7. **Dr. G. Karunanithi,** Professor and Head, Department of Sociology, Manonmaniam Sundaranar University Tirunelveli – 627 012, Tamilnadu, India.
8. **Dr. S. Maria John,** Reader and Research Advisor, Department of Commerce, Cardamom Planters' Association College, Bodinayakanur – 625 513, Tamilnadu.
9. **Dr. Mrs. A.Mary Grace,** S.G. Lecturer in History, J.A. College for women (autonomous), Mother Teresa Women's University, Periyakulam 625 601, Theni District.

10. **Dr. S.Narayana Rajan,** Reader, Department of Business Administration, Aditanar College of Arts and Science, Virapandian patnam, Tiruchendur, Thoothukudi District, Tamilnadu – 628 216.

11. **Mr. A.Nilasco Arputharaj,** Doctoral Research Scholar in Management, Madurai Kamaraj University, Madurai-625018, Tamilnadu.

12. **Mr. L.T. O. Prakash,** Research Associate, Centre for Study of Social Exclusion and Inclusive Policy, Manonmaniam Sundaranar University, Tirunelveli – 627 012.

13. **Dr. Mrs A.Padrakali,** S.G Lecturer in Commerce, A.P.C. Mahalaxmi College for Women, Thoothukudi – 628 001, Tamilnadu.

14. **Dr. S.W.P. Prabakaran,** Assistant Project Manager (Livelyhood), TNEPRP-DRDA, District Collectrate, Tirunelveli-627 008.

15. **Dr. A.Selva Kumar,** Reader in Commerce, Pope's College, Sawyerpuram – 628 251, Thoothukudi District, Tamilnadu.

16. **Mrs. J.Shobana,** Lecturer, Vidyasagar College of Arts & Science, Udumalpet – 642 126, Tamilnadu.

17. **Dr. Mrs. Shobana Nelasco,** Reader in Economics, Fatima College, Madurai – 625 018, Tamilnadu.

1

A Micro Study of Weavers and Weaving in Chinnalpatti

Dr. P. Anandharajakumar*

Abstract

India is a land of diversity and famous for unity in its rich cultural heritage. Handloom industry forms part of the Indian culture and tradition. Handloom is a household industry, spread through the length and breadth of the country. In terms of contribution to economic development, particularly in rural India, handloom industry assumes significance next only to agriculture. At present about 16 million people are solely dependent on handloom sector and another equal number in various associated industries. The need to promote handloom industry arises more on social obligation than on economic advantage. For millions handloom is not only the economic pursuit, but a way of life also. The handloom industry is largely household-based, carried out with labour contributed by the entire family. It is dispersed; spread across thousands of villages and towns in the country. The industry also exhibits considerable diversity in terms of products, organizational base, as well as its

* **Lecture in Rural Development (SS), Department of Rural Development, Gandhigram Rural University, Gandhigram.**

relations between actors within the production structure. This study attempts to provide a field appraisal of the industry.

Introduction

The handloom sector occupies a distinct and unique place in the Indian rural economy, besides being the largest generator of non-farm rural employment. The handloom industry is largely household-based, carried out with labor contributed by the entire family. It is dispersed, spread across thousand of villages and small towns in the country. The industry also exhibits considerable diversity in terms of products, organizational base, as well as in relations between actors within the production structure. The diversity is not reflected in the aggregate data on the industry. It is often such aggregate data, which from the basis not only for people's impressions about the industry, but also in attempts to formulate policies for the sector. The diversity of conditions that characterizes weavers and weaving in Tamilnadu are depicted.

Profile of Handloom Sector in Tamilnadu

The textile industry, which encompasses the organized mill sector, the unorganized decentralized sector consisting of handlooms, khadi and powerlooms, plays a crucial role in the Indian economy today. Taken together, it contributes to 8 per cent of GDP, 20 per cent of industrial production, 35 per cent of export earnings and employs around 38 million persons. The Handloom industry exhibits extreme diversity in terms of products, modes of production, as well as in relations within the production structure. Aggregate data does not reveal the grassroots level realities. What is needed is a realistic appraisal of the industry.

The handloom sector, contrary to the general notion that its share of production has declined, however, has stabilized around 20 per cent for the past two to three decades. At present it stands at 18.75 per cent of the total cloth production. The major contribution of handloom sector is however in terms of providing employment to 124 lakhs people and thus stands next to agriculture. Out of this, 60 per cent are women, 12 per cent SCs and 20 per cent STs. There are 38.91 lakhs handlooms in India.

Though its share in total textile exports is 10 per cent, its labour intensive character, decentralized nature and optimum utilization of scarce capital resources give it a unique position in the Indian economy. It weaves a range of fibres like cotton, silk, tussar, jute, wool and synthetic blends.

As per the 1995-96 Handloom Census, there are 34.86 lakh Handlooms in India, out of which 4.13 lakh Handlooms are in Tamilnadu which provide employment to 6.08 lakh workers. Out of 4.13 lakh handlooms in Tamilnadu, 2.19 lakh handlooms are functioning with 1117 Handloom Weaver's Cooperative Societies and the remaining 1.94 lakh looms are outside of the cooperative fold.

During the year 2005-06, the annual sales of handloom cloth by Tamilnadu is Rs. 1800 crore, of which, the sales made by handloom cooperatives is Rs. 719.63 crore. The average annual export of handloom cloth by Tamilnadu is Rs. 875 crore, of which export sales by Handloom cooperatives is Rs. 264.36 crore.

The Department of Handlooms has encouraged the handloom weavers' cooperative societies to produce marketable/exportable varieties and suitable action plan has been given to the societies, so as to increase the sales and also to earn profit. The Department has also encouraged the societies for product diversification and design development.

Due to the above measures taken by the Department, the number of profitable societies have increased to 850 during the year 2006-07 from the level of 760 in 2005-06.

The Table 1.1 clearly shows that handloom sector in terms of cloth production, the state of Tamilnadu stands first. In terms of number of weavers and handlooms it stands second position at the all India level.

Table 1.1: No. of Handlooms, Handloom Cloth Production and Concentration of Weavers in Tamilnadu

Item	*All India*	*Tamilnadu*	*Position of Tamilnadu*
Handlooms (in lakh)	34.86	4.13	2
Handloom Cloth Production (Bn. Sq. Mt.)	6.00	0.7	1
Handloom Cloth Production (Rs. in crores)	18000	2500	1
Weavers (in lakh)	65.50	6.08	2

Source: Handlooms, Handicrafts, Textiles and Khadi Department, Govt. of Tamilnadu, 2007.

Table 1.2: Handloom Clusters in Tamil Nadu

S. No.	*Name of the Circle*	*Clusters*
1.	Thiruvallur	R.K. Pettai, Pallipet, Tiruttani, and Ellapuram
2.	Salem	Ammpet, Kondalampatti, Attayampatti, Vasavasi and Paupparapatti
3.	Nagercoil	Vadasery, Colachel, Karungal and Palliyadi
4.	Tiruchendgode	Rasipuram, Mallasamudram, Komarapalayam and Edappadi
5.	Thiruvarur	Ammaiyappan and Mannargudi
6.	Viridhunagar	Aruppukottai, Sundarapandiam, Srivilliputhur and Rajapalayam
7.	Erode	Chennaimalai, Bhavani, Gobi and Erode Kanchi Koil
8.	Karur	Karur
9.	Kancheepuram	Kancheepuram, Pallipet and Ponneri
10.	Paramakudi	Paramakudi, Emesneswaram and Karaikudi
11.	Dindigul	Chinnalapatti and Palani
12.	Vellore	Vellore, Gudiyattam, Arni and Thiruvannamalai
13.	Cuddalore	Kurinjipadi, Bhuvanagiri and Vilupuram

(Contd...)

S. No.	Name of the Circle	Clusters
14.	Madurai	Madurai, T. Kunnathuyr and Andipatty
15.	Trichy	Woraiyur and Manamedu
16.	Kumbakonam	Kumbakonam, Thirubuvanam and Jeyankondan.
17.	Coimbatore	Coimbatore, Sirumugai and Pollachi
18.	Tirunelveli	Kallidaikurihi and Sankarankoil

Source: Handlooms, Handicrafts, Textiles and Khadi Department, Govt. of Tamilnadu, 2007.

Handlooms Under the Cooperative Sector

Handloom industry in India is the most important, ancient, traditional cottage industry which is providing employment to large number of people in rural areas and semi-urban areas. Handloom industry in Tamilnadu plays an important role in improving economic conditions of the rural poor by providing employment for more than 4.29 lakh weaver households and about 11.64 lakh weavers.

In Tamilnadu, 2.11 lakh handlooms are functioning in 1247 handloom weavers cooperative societies as on 28.02.2005 and the remaining looms are outside the purview of cooperative sector. Out the 1247 handloom weavers' societies, 1169 are cotton weavers' cooperative societies and the remaining 78 are silk weavers' cooperative societies.

The handloom weavers' cooperative societies mostly exist in rural and semi-urban areas, where there is large concentration of handloom weavers. All the development and welfare schemes meant for weavers are implemented through these societies by the Governments.

The handloom weavers cooperative societies have produced 1083.26 lakh metres of handloom cloth valued at Rs. 559.72 crore and sold handloom goods to the extent of Rs. 696.58 crore during the year 2004-05. There is an increase of sale of handloom cloth worth Rs. 121.97 crore in 2004-05 over the sales made during the years 2003-04. The number of handloom weavers' cooperative societies working on profit has been increased from 527 during the year 2003-04 to 601 during the year 2004-05.

Marketing is the major factor for the performance of the handloom weavers' cooperative societies. To capture the consumer market, production of marketable/exportable varieties has been given to the societies depending upon the market trend, so as to increase the sales.

Welfare Schemes Implemented by the Department of Handloom through Weavers' Cooperative

The following schemes of Governments are implemented through cooperative societies for the benefit of handloom weavers:

- Cooperative Handloom Weavers Savings and Security Scheme (at the time to retirement).
- Bunkar Bima Yojana Scheme (Insurance Scheme)
- Weavers House-cum-Work Shed Scheme (better work environment)
- Work Shed Scheme
- Health Package Scheme (Medical assistance)
- Cooperative Handloom Weavers Family Pension Scheme
- Cooperative Handloom Weavers Old Age Pension Scheme (after 60 years of age)

For availing the benefits under the above mentioned schemes, the handloom weavers attached with cooperative societies can approach the President of the weaver's cooperative society in the respective area of the Assistant Director of Handlooms and Textiles in the respective circle notified by the Government of Tamilnadu.

Besides, the Government of Tamilnadu has established Tamilnadu Handloom Weavers Cooperative Society Limited (Co-optex), Tamilnadu Handloom Development Corporation Limited, and Tamilnadu Zari Limited in order to render possible assistance to the weavers of cooperative societies.

Steps Taken by the Government of Tamilnadu to Enhance the Performance of Handloom Sector

The steps have been initiated by the Government of Tamilnadu in view of enhancing the performance of handloom industry.

- Free Distribution of Sarees and Dhotis Scheme to the people living below poverty line in rural and urban areas for Pongal festival.
- Special rebate without any ceiling to the customers.
- Insurance Scheme.
- Introduction of New Designs.
- Free Supply of Uniforms to School Children.
- Conduct of District Level Exhibitions.
- Production of Export-Oriented items such as bed liner, bed spreads, table liner, aprons, curtains, Teri-towels, kitchen linen, napkins, floor mats, etc.
- Special projects under SGSY for the purpose of capacity building, training, design development, skill upgradation, value addition, technology upgraduation, marketing, etc.
- Training to weavers for upgradation of skills improving designs in order to compete with the mills and powerloom sectors.
- Restructuring of Co-optex.

Issues in the Handloom Sector

The handloom sector occupies a distinct and unique place in the Indian economy, besides being the largest generator of non-farm rural employment. While available statistics indicate an economic sector of considerable size, there is still immense space for expansion. The handloom sector is indeed capable of exponential growth, with proper identification of its needs, a reasonable level of resource input and structural attention. Nevertheless, this sector is faced with innumerable problems, which ultimately hampers the performance. The major issues in this regard are discussed hereunder.

Table 1.3: Handloom Development Schemes Implemented by the Department of Handloom–Tamilnadu

S. No.	*Scheme*	*Activity*
1.	Rebate Subsidy Scheme	In order to promote the sale of Handloom cloth produced by the handloom weaver's cooperative societies, 20 rebate subsidies is provided by the Government on the sale of handloom cloth throughout the year.
2.	Free supply of Uniform Scheme	One set of uniform is provide to the school children in standards I to VIII covered under Nutritious Meal Programme. The cloth required for the Free Supply of Uniform Scheme is being produced by the weavers' cooperative societies. This scheme provided regular employment to about 12,000 weavers in the Cooperative sector.
3.	Free distribution of Dhotis and Sarees	Under this scheme, one polycot saree/dhoti is provided to the poor people during the Pongal festival. About 2.22 crore poor people are being benefited under this scheme. Cloths required under this scheme are being produced by the Weavers' Cooperative Societies.
4.	Deen Dayal Hathkargha Potash Yojana	Subsidy is given by the central and state government towards margin money assistance, supply of new looms and accessories, providing infrastructure facilities, training, designs, publicity and marketing incentive or rebate.

(Contd...)

S. No.	*Scheme*	*Activity*
5.	Interest Subsidy	The Cooperative Central Bank and Tamilnadu State Apex Cooperative Bank provide cash credit facilities to the Weavers Cooperative Societies at the Bank rate. The Government provides 3 per cent interest subsidy to the primary weaver's cooperative societies enabling them to avail concessional rate of interest.
6.	Enforcement of Handloom (Reservation of Articles for Production) Act, 1985	To protect the interest of the handloom weavers, a separate enforcement wing with headquarters at Chennai and 5 field level offices at Madurai, Salem, Tiruchegode, Erode and Tiruppur have been established. Any complaint received regarding the violation of this Act will be taken up and will be pursued against the persons violating the Act.

(A) Policy of Reservation

Since the days of independence, many regulations were imposed on both mills and powerlooms to protect the handlooms from their unequal competitions. The most important among these was the reservation of products for the exclusive production of handlooms. However, the reservation introduced for 8 items in 1950 was not very effective. Out of these 8, 5 items were reserved for both handlooms and small powerloom units. And studies point out that by 1974, almost 90 per cent of the powerloom units fell into the category of 'small' with less than 5 looms and the reservation actually benefited these powerloom units than handlooms. To correct this, the Handloom Reservation Act of 1985, reserving 22 items for the exclusive production of handlooms was introduced. However, it could not be implemented till 1993 due to the legal dispute posed by the mill and powerloom lobbies. Serious threat to handlooms comes from powerlooms rather than mills. Despite the demands of weavers the Reservation Act has ever been implemented efficiently.

(B) Competition from Powerlooms

Another cause of concern is the phenomenal growth of the number of powerlooms despite all regulation. The Sivaraman Committee observed that between 1963 and 1974 the overall growth rate of powerlooms sector was 9.67 per cent and between 1975 and 1982-83 was 11.7 per cent. In numerical terms, the growth was phenomenal, an addition of 2.3 lakhs new cotton powerlooms to the 1.93 lakh powerlooms already existing on 1975, with the overall addition of around 2.9 lakhs powerlooms, the total tall going up to 6 lakhs. Today, authorized powerlooms stand at 16.55 lakhs with the total being 34 lakhs inclusive of the unauthorized one.

(C) Availability of Yarn

Non-availability of sufficient yarn in the form of hanks has been the bane of handloom industry. The mills were supposed to deliver 50 per cent of their total yarn production in the form of hanks to handlooms. Abid Hussain Committee observed that this was to the tune of only 40 per cent. However, data from 1988-89 onwards show that it has always been around 22-24 per cent. The rise in prices of yarn of 40s and 60s count used by majority of weavers by 86.95 per cent and 128.57 per cent in 1985-90 has been attributed to the non-fulfillment of hank yarn obligation by mills. This can also be attributed to the export of yarn in the 20s and 40s count without taking into consideration the domestic requirement.

(D) Implementing of Welfare Schemes

With regard to welfare schemes, there is no dearth of schemes introduced at the State and Central Government level. A closer look at the compendium of handloom schemes and the implementation agency would reveal that majority of them are applicable only to weavers in the co-operative societies or to weavers who will be able to organize into societies or have across with the apex societies. Thus, there is no justification for the contending argument to discontinue all concessions to handlooms, as it has not led to the growth of the industry.

(E) Absence of Reliable Database

Paucity of reliable data with respect to number of looms or number of weavers or productivity is another major shortcoming of the handloom sector. Till 1964, the production of decentralized sector, except khadi, was computed on the assumption that 90 per cent of the free yarn delivered by the mills is consumed by this sector and the share of handlooms was computed on the assumption that 76 per cent of the yarn was consumed by the latter. The number of weavers is often arrived at by multiplying the number of looms by an employment co-efficient. Likewise, there is also difference of opinion in the calculation of dormant and idle looms especially while taking into account the domestic looms of Northeastern India.

(F) Technological Issues

Hand weaving has been associated, especially in the post-impendent policy formulations, with notions of 'cultural heritage', 'ancient', and 'traditional', industry in the country. In this rhetoric, its significance as an indigenous technology was often forgotten. On the basis of their structure, handlooms can be divided into: (a) primitive looms, (b) pit looms – throw shuttle and fly shuttle and (c) frame looms. In the name of technological upgradation, since early Five Year Plans, it was envisaged to convert pit looms into frame looms. The disadvantage of frame loom is that it occupies more space and is not easy to operate due to increased vibrations while weaving. Moreover, it also costs much more than a pit loom. Since 1985, technological upgradation of handlooms has been synonymous with the conversion of handlooms into power looms.

Field Realities: Data Analysis

Chinnalapatti, which is located 11 kilometres from Dindigul town on the Madurai-Dindigul National Highways is known for its flourishing handloom industry. Art-Silk Sarees and Sungudi produced in Chinnalappatti are famous throughout India by the name of chinnalapattu. More than 1000 families are traditionally engaged in this industry. Data collected from the weavers (50 weavers chosen ramdomly) in Chinalapatti are presented in Table 1.4.

Table 1.4: Socio-Economic Profile of Sample Weavers in Chinnalapatti

S. No.	*Particulars*	*No. of respondents*	*%*
1.	**Age Group**		
	30-50 years	35	70
	Above 50 years	15	30
2.	**Caste Group**		
	Chettiar (Devanga)	45	90
	Sourashtra	05	10
3.	**Educational Level**		
	Illiterates	19	38
	Primary School	18	36
	Secondary Level	13	26
4.	**Family Size**		
	1-3 members	18	36
	3-5 members	30	60
	Above 5 members	02	04

(Contd...)

S. No.	*Particulars*	*No. of respondents*	*%*
5.	**Family Type**		
	Nuclear Family	41	82
	Joint Family	09	18
6.	**Monthly Income (all sources)**		
	Below Rs. 2000	24	48
	Rs. 2000-4000	20	40
	Above Rs. 4000	06	12
7.	**Housing Type (rented and own)**		
	Tiled House	31	62
	Concrete House	19	38

Source: Field data.

The Table 1.4 shows the personal profile of sample weavers drawn for the present study. The details covered in the table would help us to understand nature of weaving occupation in the present-day situation.

Of the 50 weavers selected for study, 70 per cent of them were in the age group of 35-50 years. Only 30 per cent of them have crossed 50 years. It is a fact in the handloom weaving sector that the work efficiency of weavers normally declines when they cross 50 years of age due to eye sight problem. The families in the study area used to initiate adults in the weaving profession any time after 20 years of age so that they could work at least 25-30 years and earn for the remaining days of future.

Unlike in other parts of Tamilnadu, in Chinnalapatti town majority of the families engaged in weaving belonged to Chettiar caste (Devanga). Of the toal number of weavers studied, 90 per cent of them belonged to the above mentioned caste. Only 10 of them were from Sourashtra community. Devanga Chettiar community has been working in the handloom weaving sector for the past 3 to 4 generations together. Neverthless, of late people from the above caste have developed unwillingness to continue in the same profession due to risks and other precarious conditions experienced in the recent past in the handloom sector.

Education attainment by the weavers has a direct relationship with the skill that they develop further for the betterment of profession. In this regard, it was interesting to note that 62 percent of them got educated at various levels. However, illiterate weavers constituted 38 per cent, which is a considerable proportion to the total number of weavers' families selected for this study. But realizing the consequences of not studying before, most of the weavers in Chinnalapatti have admitted their wards in schools and colleges so that they could take up some other profession in the future. Ultimately the weaving communities in the study are attempting to delink their children from weaving profession.

Size of the family matters such as far as weaving profession is concerned, more number of members in a family would obviously mean more hands for working. This further helps in generating sufficient income. However, the weavers today are finding very difficult to earn income due to dominance of powerloom sector.

Emergence and effective survival of powerloom sector poses a serious threat to the survival of families engaged in weaving profession. However, it is found in this study that 60 per cent of weaving families had 3-5 members in their families. Active involvement of at least 2-3 adult members in weaving alone would help the weavers to manage their survival given the difficulties experienced in the handloom sector today. Joint family system (18 per cent) is still prevalent among Devanga Chettiar community for this same reason.

Data on average monthly income earned by the weavers showed that a vast majority of them (88%) have earned below Rs. 4000. This income was mainly derived from weaving cloths. Weavers those who have engaged in 'design saree' weaving got more income comparatively. However, design saree making takes more time. Weaving a cotton saree fetches only about Rs. 150 to a weaver. At least three days are needed to make a saree. Which means on an average a weaver would get Rs. 50 per day. This is less than the minimum wage prescribed.

Regarding the condition of housing among the weavers in Chinnalapatti town 62 per cent of them were residing in the tiled houses. Concrete houses constituted only 38 per cent. Most of the weavers staying in the concrete houses paid rent to the respective owners. These weavers were finding very difficult to pay rental amount. It was pathetic to note that some of families were evicted by the owners for non-payment of rent continuously.

As the profession of weaving become more and more complicated in a globalized atmosphere with the advent of powerloom sector, the weavers are extremely finding it difficult to meet both the ends. This is the situation of weavers today in Chinnalapatti. But, the condition of weavers attached to cooperative weaving societies are far better, as they are able to enjoy benefits from the schemes announced by the governments for weavers now and then. For instance, only 12 per cent of weavers interviewed for this study informed that they have got admitted as members in weavers cooperative society.

Table 1.5: Work Profile of Weavers in Chinnalapatti

S.No.	*Particulars*	*No. of respondents*	*%*
1.	**No. of Looms owned**		
	1-3 Looms	47	94
	3-5 Looms	03	06
2.	**Type of Looms**		
	Pit Loom		
	(a) Ordinary	07	08
	(b) Jacquard	20	24
	Frame Loom		
	(a) Ordinary	33	39
	(b) Jacquard	24	29
3.	**Type of yarn used**		
	Kora Silk	40	80
	Silk	03	06
	Cotton	07	14
4.	**Membership in Weavers Society**		
	Registered as members	06	12
	Non-members	44	88
5.	**No. of days required to make one piece of cloth**		
	2-4 days	40	80
	4-6 days	08	16
	6-8 days	02	04

(Contd...)

S.No.	Particulars	No. of respondents	%
6.	**Advance borrowed from local agents**		
	Rs. 2000-4000	23	46
	Rs. 4001-6000	12	24
	Rs. 6000 and above	02	04
	Not borrowed	13	26
7.	**Health problems reported**		
	Body & Joints pain	39	58
	Eye sight problems	20	40
	Heart diseases	19	38
	Ulcer	16	32
	Piles & gastric related	40	80
8	**Working House**		
	6.00 AM to 6.00 PM	44	88
	7.30 AM to 6.00 PM	06	12

Source: Filed data.

It is a well known fact that the weavers in India are put to lot of difficulties due to the dominance of powerloom sector. The working and living conditions of weavers are pathetic. For example, the weavers in Komarapalayam, Pallipalayam and a cluster of villages in Namakkal district of Tamilnadu were forced to sell their kidneys due to poverty and detained in powerloom units as bonded labourers.

Further, it was revealed that the weavers had sold their kidneys to wipe off the debts and advances incurred by them at the time of their employment. The high level team which studied the problem indicated that bonded labour system was prevailing in many of the powerloom centres functioning in Namakkal district (*The Hindu*, January 24, 2008).

The work related issues are analysed in Table 1.5. The above analysis would help us in understanding various issues involved in the handloom sector in a particular context. Only vital information were sought from the sample weavers.

Looms Under Practice

There are different types of loom existing in general. Such looms are primitive looms, pit looms, fly shuttle pit looms and frame looms. In Chinnalapatti town both the pit and frame looms are used by the weavers.

Pit looms are of two kinds—throw shuttle and fly shuttle. Until the invention of fly shuttle in England in the 18th century, the throw shuttle was the most prevalent loom. Famous throw shuttle pit looms are Gadwal looms, Jamadani looms, Balaramapuram looms, Banaras looms, Chanderi looms, Aurangabad Himru looms, and Kanjeevaram looms.

In the study area majority of weavers (94%) were maintaining 1-3 looms in their respective places. Further, it is revealed by them that 68 per cent of weavers were maintaining frame looms. Pit looms were maintained by remaining weavers. Among the pit loom owners, jacquard type were more in numbers than ordinary type. Frame looms can weave heavy furnishing material, bed sheet of greater warp (upto 100 – 110" width), towels, dress material, striped check material, gauze cloth, and so on.

Yarn Used

Yarn is being received from a commission agent based at Palani. Of the 50 weavers covered under this study, 80 per cent of them use Kora Silk followed by Cotton (14%) and Silk (6%). The weavers complain of price escalation, poor quality and inadequate yarn supply. In addition to these, the weavers are to pay commission to person designated as "agents" for bringing yearn to them. Majority of weavers weave only Kora Pattu, Cotton Sarees and Dhoti (Kerala model).

Pre-loom processes are mostly carried out by the workers engaged by the weavers for wage. This process takes normally 3-5 days in a week. For the purpose of warp joining and pound winding, an amount of Rs. 100 is paid for 8 sarees (i.e., one pound). The weavers get an amount of Rs. 955 of remanufacturing 8 sarees besides all other sundry expenses related to weaving.

Regarding the number of days needed to weave one saree, it was opinioned by majority of weavers (80%) that they took 3-4 days. Design saree making takes considerable time extending even upto 1 ½ months for a pound.

Cooperative Societies for Weavers

With a view to providing uninterrupted employment to weavers, the Government of Tamilnadu has promoted work-shed type industrial cooperative societies for weavers. With an object of boosting the sale of handloom cotton and silk fabrics produced by the primary weavers cooperative societies, the Government has seven marketing complex in different parts of the state. Savings and security schemes for cooperative handloom weavers are being implemented since 1975-76.

However, it is found in this study that only 12 per cent of weavers interviewed, informed that they have entrolled them as members of weavers cooperative society. The weavers those who have entrolled as members in the society were better placed in several aspects of weaving profession. Members used to get advance from the society. Weaver members are able to take maximum advantage of schemes that are being implemented by the Governments for their welfare unlike non-members. Which means, those weavers who have entrolled themselves as members of cooperative societies were placed better than their counterparts.

Advance Borrowal

Despite all the claims of subsidies to the handloom sector, the amount of institutional credit that is made available to weavers is abysmally low. While banks have an inbuilt bias against small producers, the credit facilities available to the cooperative societies are far from adequate. This situation leads to indebtedness among weavers. Invariably weavers end up indebted to the local moneylenders or master weavers.

As per this study, a vast majority of weavers interviewed (74 %) have borrowed advance from the local moneylenders and majority of them have not paid the amount back and hence they are under the trap of indebtedness. Now both the principal and interest amounts accumulated and majority of them are unable to clear their dues. In order to improve this condition, self-help groups among weavers in Chinnalapatti may be promoted.

Health Problems

With view to ameliorating some of the health problems among handloom weavers, a scheme "Health Package Scheme for Handloom Weavers' with 10 per cent central subsidy which is inclusive of providing assistance from primary health care, has been introduced by the Government of India from the year 1992-93. Under this scheme facilities such as (a) reimbursement of cost of medicine, (b) reimbursement of cost of eye test and spectacles, (c) supply of drinking water, (d) maternity benefit for women, (e) compensation for sterilization, and (f) infrastructure for primary health centres.

Most of the weavers interviewed under this study informed of health problems, such as Body and Joints pain (58%), Eye-sight problems (40%), Heart diseases (38%), Ulcer (32%), Piles and gastric related problems (80%). These weavers (88%) are working at least 12 hours a day i.e., from 6.00 AM to 6.00 PM. Because of lengthy working hours the weavers are subjected to most of the problems mentioned above. Sitting in the same position poses serious threat to their health in terms of problems like piles and back bone pain.

Summary

The twentieth century saw the emergence of mill industry as well as the decentralized powerloom sector which have now become the serious competitors to the handlooms. Many committees, appointed by the Government, recommended that powerloom be allowed to acquire a paramount position in the textile economy of India. These committees have questioned the long-term viability of handlooms and argued for the removal of regulations in total, the permission for planned expansion of powerlooms marked official recognition of the role of powerlooms in India.

As indicated earlier, the serious threat to handlooms come from powerlooms rather than mills. It is argued that powerlooms are result of expansion of successful handloom weavers. In addition, low order head costs per unit of output, low wages due to lack of unionization, small size of the units enabling it remains outside the ambit of any protective labour legislation give them a competitive edge over both mills and handlooms. A larger question to be considered would be of the agents of intervention: What should be the role of the state towards these issues and how would the weavers be enabled to engage in weaving profession in spite of massive growth of powerloom sector? Aspects such as credit needs, cooperatisation, marketing facilities, health development schemes, export promotion, product reservation etc, would go a long way in addressing the issues raised in this paper.

REFERENCES

1. Seemanthini Nirnajana and Soumya Vinayan (2001): Report on Growth and Prospects of the Handloom Industry, Planning Commission of India, GOI, New Delhi.
2. Anjaneyulu (1990): *Financial Management in the Cooperative Handloom Industry*, Classifiable Publishing Company, New Delhi.
3. Arulanandhan (1979): *"A Study of Handloom Industry in Tamilnadu"*, Unpublished Ph.D thesis, Madurai Kamaraj University, Madurai (TN).
4. Rama Mohan Rao. K (1990): *Development of Handloom Industry*, Discovery Publishing Company, New Delhi.
5. Venkatesh (1995): *"Handloom in Tamilnadu: Weaving New Vistas, Cooperator"*, July, Vol. 32 (1), New Delhi.
6. Venu Gopal Rao. K and Chandrasekar (1998): Problems of Handloom Industry, *Kurukshetra* – March, Vol. 56 (6), New Delhi.

2

A Study on the Conditions of Quarry Workers at Vagaikulam Area in Thoothukudi Distirct

V. Duraisingh*

Abstract

Stone quarry workers form an unorganized sector of industry scattered all over Tamilnadu. Various procedures and operations are involved in this work viz. stone cutting, loading and crushing. Quarry industry has been well familiar and also a very high degree of respiratory morbidity is associated with this industry. Moreover, as the workers are exposed to silica dust over a long term, suffering from chronic cough and large lung function injury is found in this group of workers. The present study was, therefore, designed to evaluate the conditions of stone quarry workers.

Introduction

Quarry workers, sometimes known as quarry operatives, work in quarries throughout the country. As stated, the building industry relies on quarries to supply crushed stone and sand.

* **Lecturer in Economics, Manonmaniam Sundaranar University, Tirunelveli – 628 012, Tamil Nadu.**

Modern quarrying is a mechanical process involving large, powerful excavating, transporting and crushing equipment. Machine operators work with heavy plant machinery such as excavators, draglines and cranes. Plant and process operators are employed on crushers, screening plant and graders, drilling, setting up and operating drilling equipment. Maintenance workers, fitters, mechanics and electricians work on plant and vehicle maintenance. Shotfirers work with explosives, technicians work in laboratories on quality control or recording site samples. Quarry workers normally work a 48 hour week, with overtime and shift work being very common.

Stone quarry workers form an unorganized sector of industry scattered all over Tamilnadu. They work in quarries and open cast mines, excavating rock and minerals and processing them to make products for industry, for example, quarrying limestone for cement production, crushing rock to make stone chippings and aggregates used in road construction, extracting clay for brick-making, and slate for roofing. There are various duties within a quarry, such as working with heavy plant machinery such as excavators, draglines and cranes, operating processing equipment like rock crushers and stone graders, setting up and using drilling equipment, carrying out maintenance on vehicles and machinery, setting and detonating explosives, known as 'shotfiring' and transporting materials with large tipper and dumper trucks.

Review of Literature

Ghotkari et al. summarised that the workers employed in stone quarries, which is an unorganised sector of industry, are exposed to variable silica dust concentration at their work place. A very large extent of respiratory morbidity and lung function impairment is observed in this group of employees. A cross-sectional study was carried out to study the respiratory morbidity and diseases involving lung function in this group. This study has found 32.5 per cent prevalence of respiratory morbidity in stone quarry workers, on the basis of radiological appearance. However, no case of silicosis was detected. The impairment of lung function was significantly associated with increasing age, duration of dust exposure, smoking status and presence of chronic obstructive airways disease on radiological appearance. However, the measured dust concentration levels were found to be in permissible range. Thus, it can be concluded from this study that even low dust level exposure for longer duration can result in malfunction of lungs. Hence, stone quarry workers, because of their occupational exposure to silica dust, are at increased risk of lung diseases. (Ghotkari, 1995).

A study of silicosis was conducted in 1992-94 by Mathur, which included a sample of 458 sandstone quarry workers of Jodhpur, to find out the pattern and predictors of mortality among sandstone quarry workers. Houses of all workers were visited and the worker's status was recorded. Standardized mortality ratio (for all causes of death) was calculated. Cox proportional hazard model was applied to study the association of different variables with mortality. Total 97.8 per cent workers could be followed, of whom, 10.9 per cent had died (SMR = 1.72; 95% CI 1.23 - 2.19). The average age at the time of death of the deceased was 51.8 ± 12.5 years. Mortality was higher among silicotics (SMR = 2.54; 95% CI 1.43-3.66), smokers (SMR = 1.83; 95% CI 1.27 - 2.39), and those showing mixed abnormality in pulmonary function test (SMR = 2.73; 95% CI 1.24 - 4.21) (Mathur, 2005).

Western Regional Centre, Goa, reported that the study dealt with how productivity could be increased with minimum investment in capital and human training. The three main causes for concern identified were the changing land-use, the inhalation of dust and hydrocarbon fumes by the machine operators and the practice of leaving large open holes in the ground without back filling, which in the monsoon turned into death traps for the pedestrians. (Western Regional Centre, Goa).

Objectives

1. To study the social conditions of quarry workers;
2. To analyse the economic condition;
3. To know the problems of quarry workers;
4. To suggest policy measures.

Methodology

The survey method carried out at stone quarries situated in Vagaikulam area, 12 kms west of Thoothukudi city. There are about seven such unorganised stone quarries situated in this area. However, two quarries from this area were selected for the study. The subjects for this study consisted of 50 workers from these stone quarries.

Thoothukudi Profile

Thoothukudi district carved out of the erstwhile Tirunelveli district in 1986 has certain rare features. The mixed landscape of the sea and the theri (waste) lands has imbibed some special traits in the character of the sons of the soil. The area of the district is 4,621 sq.k.m. and the population is 15,72,273. The district has three revenue divisions, eight taluks, twelve blocks, three municipalities, nineteen town panchayats and 468 revenue village. Seven constituencies are in the district. The climate is hot and dry. The district has a coastal line of 163.5 kms. and territorial waters covering thousands of hectares. The district, particularly in and around Thoothukudi, is the major salt producer in the state and contributes 30 per cent of the total salt production of the country. Changing economic scenario has added to the development of the district. The main food crop in this district is paddy. Out of the total area of 459,054 hectares, 171,815 hectares are brought under the cultivation of different crops which is nearly 37 per cent of total area of the district.

The total value of Rs. 79,63,055 rough stones are produced in the year 2005-06. The production and value of major minerals in Thoothukudi district for the year 2005-06 are presented in the Table 2.1.

Table 2.1: Production and Value of Major Minerals in Thoothukudi District (2005-06)

Name of the Minerals	*Quality (Units)*	*Value (in Rs.)*
Rough Stone	1,10,598	79,63,055
Garnet Sand	1,000	2,71,44,261
Lime Stone	6,03,206	2,71,44,261
Earth	44,472	17,89,665
Gravel	88,945	40,02,536
Quailizite	542	1,62,600
Lime Shell	35	7,000
Granite	186.047 m3	2,93,025

Source: www.thotthukudi.com

The sandstone quarries in Vagaikulam area are a major source of employment in the area. These are open quarries on surface of rocky land. The workers drill holes in rocks with chisel and big hammers, but in the last few years, drilling machines are being used in most of the quarries. After drilling holes in straight line in a rock they put some explosives in holes and blast them. This breaks the rocks into huge blocks, which are then cut into long slabs or stones. This stone cutting is done manually using huge hammers. In the process of quarrying, workers are exposed to high concentrations of silica rich respirable dust. Measures of prevention of silicosis are practically not adopted by them.

Results and Discussion

All 50 workers were males. Female workers were not included in the study as very few females worked in sandstone quarries. Majority of the workers belong to the age group of 20-40 years. The annual income particulars of the stone quarry workers are listed in the Table 2.2.

Table 2.2: Income Level of the Respondents

Income Level (in Rs.)	*No. of Respondents*	*Percentage*
Below 10,000	2	4
10,000-15,000	4	8
15,000-20,000	20	40
20,000-25,000	12	24
25,000-30,000	10	20
Above 30,000	2	4
Total	**50**	**100**

Source: Field Survey.

The Table 2.2 reveals that majority (40%) of the respondents are earning an annual income between Rs. 15,000-20,000. Only two labourers (4%) are earning a maximum annual income above Rs. 30,000 and another two labourers (4%) are earning a minimum level of income below Rs. 10,000. Average income of the respondents of this study is Rs. 19,524. The income of the respondent deviate from the mean income by Rs. 5,303. The minimum income of the respondent is Rs. 7,600 and the maximum is Rs. 30,400. This implies that the inequality in incomes among the six groups of households are very less. Gini Concentration Ratio was computed. The Gini Concentration ratio is 0.3351. This confirms that the income inequality among the three groups of households is very less.

Further this study discloses that 48 per cent of the quarry labourers have been working below 10 years and maximum of 52 per cent labourers have been working more than 10 years. Also this study clearly indicated that majority of the quarry labourers are working for more than eight hours per day and working for six days per week. They normally work 48 hours per week, with overtime and shift work being very common.

Some of the workers from the quarries in Adaikalapattnam said the price of a load of stone had increased from Rs. 225 in 1996 to Rs. 430. But they had received only a marginal rise in wages from Rs. 65 to Rs. 70 in the past 10 years. Rs. 70 was given for every 125 cubic feet of stone they broke in groups of about five. On this basis, the workers received around Rs.150 a day, but there was no guarantee of work everyday.

Seven (14%) workers had discontinued their job because of their sickness. But all the workers were suffering from chronic cough and heart pain disease.

Problems Faced by Stone Quarry Workers

The stone quarry workers are facing more problems at the place of stone industry. Table 2.3 reveals the problems that have been faced by the workers in working quarry. Giving weight to various problems, it is explained.

1 – Rank = 5 points

2 – Rank = 4 points

3 – Rank = 3 points

4 – Rank = 2 points

5 – Rank = 1 point

Ranking the problem while working quarry.

Table 2.3: Problems Faced by Quarry Workers

Sources	*I*	*II*	*III*	*IV*	*V*	*Total*
Low Wages	20	8	11	5	6	50
Disease Problems	6	11	9	12	12	50
No Job Security	6	10	12	11	11	50
Hazards Work	8	8	8	12	14	50
Accident	10	13	10	10	7	50
Total	**50**	**50**	**50**	**50**	**50**	**250**

On the basis of the points given and ranks obtained, the total rank of each problem was calculated. The total rank is thus derived by the total number of respondents for each problem, to arrive at a rank. Among the five factors given in the schedule, the one, which had the highest mean score, was identified as the major problem faced by the quarry workers at the time of working in quarry.

Calculation of Garrett Mean Score

Now the Garrett Ranking Technique was employed and the influencing factor was arrived at. The Garrett Ranking Technique was adopted to identify the most influencing factor. The formula for calculating Garrett Ranking Technique was

$$\text{Present Position} = \frac{100(Rij - 0.5)}{Nj}$$

where,

Rij = Rank given for the *i*th reason by *j*th respondents

Nj = Number of factors ranked by *j*th respondents

Following Table 2.4 shows that Garrett mean score of each problem.

Table 2.4: Garrett Mean Score

Problems	*Garrett Ranking Mean Score*	*Rank*
Low Wages	27.31	I
Hazards Work	19.78	V
No Job Security	20.07	IV
Disease Problems	20.62	III
Accident	22.22	II

It is inferred from Table 2.4 that, among the various problems met by the quarry workers at the time of working in quarry, low wages is the main problem. Next the accident, disease problems is another problem that is faced by the quarry workers. No job security and hazards work are the least problems faced by the quarry workers in working stone industry. The following figure depicts the Garrett mean score.

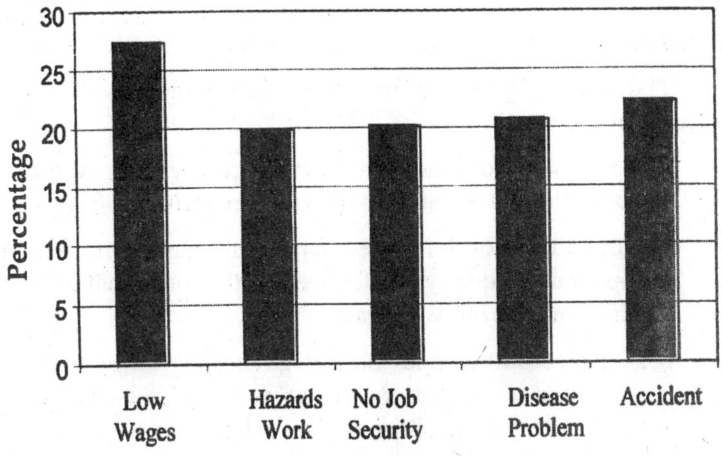

Fig. 2.1: Garrett Mean

Findings

- All 50 workers were males. Female workers were not included in the study as very few females worked in sandstone quarries.
- Majority of the workers belong to the age group of 20-40 years.
- Majority of the respondents are earning an annual income between Rs.15,000-20,000. Only two labourers are earning a maximum annual income above Rs. 30,000.
- Further this study discloses that 48 per cent of the quarry labourers have been working below 10 years and maximum of 52 per cent labourers have been working for more than 10 years.
- The workers received around Rs. 150 a day, but there was no guarantee of work everyday.
- Seven (14%) workers had discontinued their job because of their sickness. But all the workers were suffering from chronic cough and heart pain disease.
- Among the various problems met by the quarry workers at the time of working in quarry, low wages is the main problem. Next, the accident and disease problems are another problem that is faced by the quarry workers.

Suggestion

The following suggestions have been made based on the findings of the study.

- It is observed from the study that the quarry owners should adopt measures to the prevent from exposure to fine dust.
- The conditions of the stone quarry workers in this area are very poor, so the quarry workers feel that the government should interfere and fix fair wage rate.
- It is also recommended that the government may provide job-oriented training to the quarry workers and small scale industries may be established. It may be useful to reduce the unemployment problems among the quarry workers.
- Most of the households have poor asset holding. In order to strengthen their assets position, the Government should start self-employment schemes.
- Rest houses, waiting hall, medical facilities should be given to the quarry workers.

REFERENCES

1. Construction Opportunities: Quarry Worker, Quarry Worker Current Vacancies, England_UK.htm, 2007.
2. Ghotkari.V.B., Maldhure. B. R and Zodpey. S.P, Involvement of Lung and Lung Function Tests in Stone Quarry Workers, Ind. J. Tube, 1995, 42, 155, www.google.com.
3. Mathur, M.L., Pattern and Predictors of Mortality in Sandstone Quarry Workers, Desert Medicine Research Centre, Jodhpur, India, *Indian Journal of Occupational and Environmental Medicine*, 9(2), 2005, pp. 80-85, www.indian J occup. enviro.htm.
4. The Small-scale Indian Laterite Stone Quarry and Working Sector: A Case Study of Goa, Western Regional Centre, Goa, www.google.com.
5. www.thoothukudi.com.

3

Problems of Women Domestic Workers

A Study in Tirunelveli City

Dr. R. Ezhil Jasmine*

Abstract

Domestic work seems to be the last resort for the poor and disadvantaged section of women. It is considered to be a residue occupation. Employment of domestic workers has become common in Tirunelveli city where a large number of housewives are going out for jobs. The domestic workers work either full time for one employer or part time for many employers. They belong to lower stratum of the society and have to necessarily work to meet or supplement their family income. The problems of women domestic workers are multi-faceted. The workers toil from under- or non-payment of wages, lack of social security, heavy workload and indebtedness to moneylenders. In fact, they are not recognized as workers. They are the most exploited working class in India. There are no rules and regulations governing their working conditions and they remain unorganized. Above all, they do not have easy access to legal protection. The Government should take

* M.Com., M.Phil., Ph.D., Lecturer in Commerce, Government Arts College for Women, Sivagangai.
e-mail: ezhilmohan4@yahoo.co.in

effective steps to solve the problems of domestic workers by entitling them to get all benefits like that of other workers.

Introduction

Domestic service or the employment of people for wages in their employer's residence was sometimes simply called "service". Domestic workers perform domestic chores such as washing, ironing, shopping, cooking and cleaning the house. In India, in ancient times, domestic work was largely performed by 'Serfs' belonging to the 'Shudras', who were denied access to education. The emancipation of middle-class women in the late twentieth century and their entry into the professional workforce has given rise to a sharp increase in the employment of domestic workers in India. According to 1991 census, 5.76 lakh women were engaged in the domestic services industries. Due to a large gap between the urban and rural incomes and lack of employment opportunities in the countryside, even an ordinary middle class urban family could afford to employ a full-time domestic worker. As such the household workloads are shifted to the domestic workers. These workers belong to the lower stratum of the society and are often considered as cheap labour. The problems of domestic workers are complex and huge in its magnitude.

Need for the Study

Tirunelveli city is the headquarters of Tirunelveli district in the state of Tamilnadu (South India). It is a 2000 year-old city, located on the banks of the perennial Thamirabarani River. It has a population of 4,11,298 (2001 census) spread over an area of 128.65 sq.kms. Due to the high demand for domestic workers in Tirunelveli city, the people from the nearby rural villages are moving to the city to serve as domestic workers for the urban population. But there is lack of job satisfaction among the women domestic workers especially due to lack of social security, poor wages and long hours of work. Poverty and unemployment are the primary reasons for women domestic workers entering into labour market. Hence an attempt has been made to study the problems of women domestic workers in Tirunelveli city.

Objectives of the Study

The study intends to pursue the following objectives:

- To study the reasons why women domestic workers enter into labour market.
- To find out the socio-economic conditions of the women domestic workers.
- To know the occupational diseases of women domestic workers.
- To study the problems of women domestic workers.
- To study the job satisfaction of women domestic workers.

Methodology of the Study

As the domestic workers are not well conversant with social science investigations, interview schedules were administered as a primary tool for the purpose of collecting primary data from them. The interview schedule was based on the objectives and parameters of the study. Several attempts were made to interview the domestic workers in their work spot and at their homes. Some of them hesitated to respond because of the fear of termination while some others readily answered the questions. Observation sheets were also used to record relevant and useful observations. The interview schedule was pre-tested and modified (wherever necessary) before actual collection of data.

Sample Size

For the sake of the study, 124 women domestic workers were selected by adopting purposive sampling method. Due care has been taken to include samples from different parts of Tirunelveli city namely Junction area, Vannarpettai, Murugankurichi, Melapalayam, Maharajanagar, Samathanapuram, Thyagarajanagar, Perumalpuram, N.G.O. Colony, Kulavanigarpuram and other important locations.

The Table 3.1 highlights that majority of the women domestic workers (45.2%) belong to the age group of 20 to 40 years, 29.8 per cent workers belong to the age group of 40 to 60 years, 13.7 per cent workers are above 60 years and the remaining 11.3 per cent domestic workers are below 20 years.

Table 3.1: Age-wise Classification of the Domestic Workers

Sl. No.	*Age in years*	*No. of domestic workers*	*Percentage*
1.	Below 20	14	11.3
2.	20 - 40	56	45.2
3.	40 - 60	37	29.8
4.	Above 60 years	17	13.7
	Total	**124**	**100**

Source: Primary data.

The educational profile of the domestic workers is also studied and presented Table 3.2.

Table 3.2: Education-wise Classification of the Domestic Workers

Sl. No.	*Education level*	*No. of domestic workers*	*Percentage*
1.	Illiterate	2	1.6
2.	Below SSLC	81	65.3
3.	SSLC	35	28.2
4.	Higher Secondary	6	4.9
	Total	**124**	**100**

Source: Primary data.

It was found out that majority of the women domestic workers (65.3%) are educated below SSLC level, 28.2 per cent workers are SSLC holders, 4.9 per cent workers are Higher Secondary holders and 1.6 per cent workers are illiterates. A remarkable point is that they do not have awareness regarding new avenues of employment. Besides it is impossible for them to get training in any skill other than domestic work. But a few of them learn typewriting, embroidery, handicrafts and computer courses. They have a concrete plan of switching over to a better type of employment. One of the workers stated that her employer sponsors her computer education and encourages her constantly.

Table 3.3: Marital Status of the Domestic Workers

Sl. No.	*Marital status*	*No. of domestic workers*	*Percentage*
1.	Married	101	81.5
2.	Unmarried	23	18.5
	Total	**124**	**100**

Source: Primary data.

Table 3.3 shows that out of 124 domestic workers taken for the study, 81.5 per cent are married and the remaining 18.5 per cent are unmarried. Almost all the unmarried domestic workers serve on full time basis and they reside in their place of employment i.e. the house of the employers. They are young and energetic, capable of discharging any kind of domestic work. But they are extremely vulnerable to sexual abuse of various kinds. They grieve that they become the prey for each and every member of the employer's house. They are totally powerless and do not have easy access to legal protection. In fact, they are scared to disclose the roguish activities of their employers chiefly due to lack of job security.

Table 3.4: Family Size of the Domestic Workers

Sl. No.	*Size of family*	*No. of domestic workers*	*Percentage*
1.	1 to 2 members	8	6.5
2.	2 to 4 members	55	44.4
3.	4 to 6 members	49	39.5
4.	More than 6 members	12	9.6
	Total	**124**	**100**

Source: Primary data.

Table 3.4 reveals that majority of the domestic workers (44.4%) have 2 to 4 members in their families, 39.5 per cent workers have 4 to 6 members, 9.6 per cent workers have more than 6 members and only 6.5 per cent workers have 1 to 2 members in their families. Some of them are bread winners. They are widows and deserted women who had to support their families with the income they earn. Some of them have pathetic conditions in their family which includes unemployed members, drunkard husband or father, handicapped children, sick parents and over debt.

Due to the changing conditions, most of the domestic workers in Tirunelveli city prefer to live in nuclear families. Only a few of them live in joint families. Besides they have realized the importance of small family and are gradually adopting the family planning concept. The Table 3.5 presents the number of children of the domestic workers taken for the study.

Table 3.5: Number of Children of Domestic Workers

Sl. No.	*No. of children*	*No. of domestic workers**	*Percentage*
1.	1 to 2	46	45.5
2.	2 to 4	44	43.6
3.	More than 4	4	3.9
4.	No Children	7	7.0
	Total	**101**	**100**

Source: Primary data.

* Only 101 domestic workers (101/124) are married.

Majority of the domestic workers (45.5%) have 1 to 2 children, 43.6 per cent have 2 to 4 children, 3.9 per cent have more than 4 children and 7 per cent have no children. Though the domestic workers are educated only up to school level, their children are studying in schools, colleges and renowned institutes. Some of their children are studying in Engineering colleges and Polytechnic colleges on merit basis.

The study (Table 3.6) reveals that 58.1 per cent of the women domestic workers have two earning members in their family, 20.2 per cent workers have only one earning member (worker itself), 14.5 per cent workers have three earning members and 7.2 per cent workers have more than three earning members in their families. The male members of their families were mostly auto drivers, hawkers, construction workers, carpenters, peddlers, hotel employees, hospital employees and scavengers.

Table 3.6: Number of Earning Members in the Family of Domestic Workers

Sl. No:	*Earning members*	*No. of domestic workers*	*Percentage*
1.	One *	25	20.2
2.	Two **	72	58.1
3.	Three **	18	14.5
4.	More than three **	9	7.2
	Total	**124**	**100**

Source: Primary data.

* Respondent herself.

** Including the respondent.

The women domestic workers have taken up domestic work owing to various reasons. The major reasons are analyzed in the study and shown in Table 3.7.

Table 3.7: Reasons for Taking up Domestic Work

Sl. No.	*Reasons*	*No. of domestic workers*	*Percentage*
1.	Economic reason	56	45.2
2.	Bread winner	25	20.2
3.	Safe work environment	8	6.5
4.	Non-marketable skills	28	22.6
5.	Flexible working hours	7	5.6
	Total	124	100

Source: Primary data.

Economic Reason

It was found out from Table 3.7 that 45.2 per cent of the domestic workers have selected domestic work due to economic reasons. Poverty and unemployment are the basic reasons for this attitude. Guruvammal, a domestic worker in Tirunelveli city stated that her husband, who is a Plumber, seldom brings home money. Instead he spends all his earnings on smoking, drinking and eating junk food. Hence Guruvammal is forced to take up domestic work.

Bread Winners

The Table 3.7 reveals that 20.2 per cent of the workers have opted domestic work because they have no other source. They are single earners (bread winners) who entirely depend on the income from domestic work. With no social security or health coverage and very little administrative support, the domestic workers manage to survive and find their way out of hunger and homelessness.

Safe Work Environment

The Table 3.7 study shows that 6.5 per cent of the domestic workers have chosen domestic work for the sake of safe work environment. They stated that their family members leave their houses early in the morning and return only in the evening after the day's work. Hence, instead of sitting idle, they prefer to do domestic work in the houses located in surrounding area. They felt that domestic work is always safe and involves no hazards.

Non-marketable Skills

22.6 per cent of the domestic workers have opted domestic work mainly because of their non-marketable skills as per Table 3.7. They are largely people from lower castes and downtrodden families who have no access to any type of training that could open new avenues of employment. Domestic work is the only area in which they could excel.

Flexible Working Hours

The Table 3.7 shows that 5.6 per cent of the women domestic workers prefer domestic work due to flexible working hours. Especially part time domestic workers could fix their working hours according to their convenience. Most of them go back to their houses after completion of morning duty and return to work in the evening. Hence they could look after the day-to-day affairs of their own families.

Full time domestic workers could be accessed by the employers at any time irrespective of day or night. Hence it becomes difficult to identify their working hours. They have to wake up even during midnight hours especially when a guest arrives. The full time women domestic workers are prone to sexual exploitations by members of the employer's family, frequent guests, relatives, neighbours and friends.

Table 3.8: Nature of Employment of the Domestic Workers

Sl. No.	*Nature*	*No. of domestic workers*	*Percentage*
1.	Full time	19	15.3
2.	Part time	105	84.7
	Total	**124**	**100**

Source: Primary data.

Part time domestic workers have stipulated working hours. They have to be very punctual and sincere in doing the specific tasks assigned by the employers under whom they work.

Table 3.9: Number of Employers Served by the Domestic Workers (per day)

Sl. No.	*No. of employers*	*No. of domestic workers*	*Percentage*
1.	One	23	18.5
2.	Two	32	25.8
3.	Three	41	33.1
4.	Four	22	17.7
5.	More than four	6	4.9
	Total	**124**	**100**

Source: Primary data.

It is apparent from Table 3.9 that majority of the women domestic workers (33.1%) serve three employers, 25.8 per cent workers serve two employers, 18.5 per cent workers serve one employer, 17.7 per cent workers serve four employers and only 4.9 per cent workers serve more than 4 employers. Due to poor wage structure, the part time workers serve more than one employer and strive hard to earn money.

Table 3.10: Number of Hours Worked by the Domestic Workers (per day)

Sl. No.	*Working hours*	*No. of domestic workers*	*Percentage*
1.	1 to 2 hours	9	7.3
2.	2-4 hours	18	14.5
3.	4-6 hours	31	25.0
4.	6-8 hours	47	37.9
5.	Full time	19	15.3
	Total	**124**	**100**

Source: Primary data.

It is clear from the Table 3.10 that 37.9 per cent of the women domestic workers work for 6 to 8 hours per day, 25 per cent work for 4 to 6 hours, 15.3 per cent work on full time basis, 14.5 per cent work for 2 to 4 hours and 7.3 per cent work for 1 to 2 hours per day. The part time workers are fully engaged in their duties especially during morning and evening hours. They are provided snacks and meals by their employers. The full time workers are expected to work round the clock. Their typical tasks include cooking, washing, ironing, shopping and looking after the children of the employers. The employers provide them breakfast, lunch, snacks and supper.

Table 3.11: Personal Income of the Domestic Workers (per month)

Sl. No.	*Income (in Rupees)*	*No. of domestic workers*	*Percentage*
1.	Below 500	10	8.1
2.	500-1000	36	29.0
3.	1000-1500	59	47.6
4.	1500-2000	15	12.1
5.	Above 2000	4	3.2
	Total	**124**	**100**

Source: Primary data.

Table 3.11 shows that 47.6 per cent of the women domestic workers earn Rupees 1000 to Rupees 1500 per month, 29 per cent workers earn Rupees 500 to Rupees 1000, 12.1 per cent workers earn Rupees 1500 to Rupees 2000, 8.1 per cent workers earn below Rupees 500 and 3.2 per cent workers earn above Rupees 2000. In fact, most of the domestic workers stated that they seldom get their wages at the beginning of the month. One of the workers said that her employer deducts two days wages if she is absent for one day. But a few employers are found to be very prompt in wage payment.

Table 3.12: Family Income of Domestic Workers (per month)

Sl. No.	*Income (in Rupees)*	*No. of domestic workers*	*Percentage*
1.	Below 1500	33	26.6
2.	1500-3000	39	31.5
3.	3000-4500	44	35.5
4.	Above 4500	8	6.5
	Total	**124**	**100**

Source: Primary data.

It is clearly evident from Table 3.12 that 35.5 per cent of the women domestic workers have a family income of Rupees 3000 to Rupees 4500, 31.5 per cent workers have a family income of Rupees 1500 to Rupees 3000, 26.6 per cent workers have a family income below Rupees 1500 and 6.5 per cent workers have a family income above Rupees 4500. The domestic workers felt that they find it highly difficult to run their family with such a meagre income. Some of them are single earners who entirely depend on the income from domestic work.

Table 3.13: Type of Residence of the Domestic Workers

Sl. No.	*Type of residence*	*No. of domestic workers*	*Percentage*
1.	Own house	8	6.5
2.	Rented house	113	91.1
3.	Leased house	3	2.4
	Total	**124**	**100**

Source: Primary data.

Table 3.13 shows that 91.1 per cent of the domestic workers reside in rented houses, 6.5 per cent workers reside in own houses and 2.4 per cent workers reside in leased houses. The workers residing in rented houses are often forced to shift their houses. They struggle to search another house and settle down. Some times they lose their job in this process. The house rent takes away a considerable portion of their income and leaves a little residual income to meet other necessities.

Table 3.14: Expenditure Pattern of the Domestic Workers (per month)

Sl. No.	*Expenditure*	*Percentage of monthly income*
1.	House rent	26.6
2.	Grocery	50.9
3.	Clothing	0.8
4.	Loan Repayment	9.8
5.	Education	10.4
6.	Health	0.3
7.	Savings	0.7
8.	Miscellaneous	0.5
	Total	**100**

Source: Primary data.

- The expenditure of each domestic worker is converted in to percentages and averages are taken for each expenditure.

House Rent

Table 3.14 shows that domestic workers spend 26.6 per cent of their income for paying the house rent. As they work in urban area, they reside in small houses or portion of a small house which is located in a walking distance from the employer's residence. The house rent in urban locality is rather high which the domestic workers could not afford. One of the workers stated that her house owner demands rent on the first day of every month and frequently threatens her to vacate the house.

Grocery

Table 3.14 study shows that the domestic workers spend majority of their monthly income on grocery items (50.9%). Some of them buy grocery items on credit from the shops close to their residence and they settle their account in the beginning of every succeeding month. Besides they also buy rice, sugar, kerosene and wheat from ration shops.

Clothing

Most of the domestic workers are struggling with poverty so much that they can not even think of buying clothes. The employers provide them clothing especially in the event of festivals and special functions. Besides they also get free saree and dhoti (once a year) from Government of Tamilnadu (Public Distribution system) through ration cards. Hence they spend only 0.8 per cent of their income for clothing.

Loan Repayment

Paucity of finance is a challenge that characterizes the lives of all domestic workers. They borrow from moneylenders to meet unexpected expenditure or to manage a financial crisis. But they struggle hard to repay the loan with their poor income. One of the workers stated that she pays huge interest to the moneylenders for the past ten years. The study found out that 9.8 per cent of their income is spent for the purpose of repayment of loan.

Education

The domestic workers spend 10.4 per cent of their income for the education of their children. It is appreciable to note that their children are studying in schools, colleges and renowned institutes. Some of them have borrowed money from their employers for the higher education of their children.

Health

Only a negligible amount (0.3%) is spent by the domestic workers for health care. Some of them get medical treatments from Government hospitals while some other get treatments in private hospitals. A few full time workers stated that their employers reimburse the medical expenses (if any) incurred by them.

Savings

All domestic workers have the eagerness and desire to save money for their future commitments. The study shows that the workers save only 0.7 per cent (average) of their income. Especially, the full time workers save more money when compared to the part time workers.

Table 3.15: Experience of Women Domestic Workers (in years)

Sl. No.	*Experience (in years)*	*No. of domestic workers*	*Percentage*
1.	Less than 5 years	21	16.9
2.	5 – 10 years	23	18.6
3.	10–15 years	22	17.7
4.	15-20 years	32	25.8
5.	More than 20 years	26	21.0
	Total	**124**	**100**

Source: Primary source.

Table 3.15 shows that 25.8 per cent of the women domestic workers have 15 to 20 years experience, 21 per cent workers have more than 20 years experience, 18.6 per cent workers have 5 to 10 years experience, 17.7 per cent workers have 10 to 15 years experience and 16.9 per cent workers have less than 5 years experience in doing domestic work.

Occupational diseases pose a serious problem to the women domestic workers. Exposure to smoke, unhygienic methods of floor cleaning and toilet cleaning, irregular food consumption, continuous exposure to water and washing powder and lack of nutritious food causes different types of occupational diseases. Majority of the domestic workers suffer from body pain/back pain/ leg pain, anemia and ulcer. The domestic workers generally do not eat rich food. Though they work hard, they eat only one or two times a day. This affects their health to a great extent (Table 3.16).

Table 3.16: Occupational Diseases of Domestic Workers

Sl. No.	*Disease*	*No. of domestic workers*	*Percentage*
1.	Back pain/body pain/ leg pain	19	15.3
2.	Skin disease	5	4.0
3.	Anaemia	18	14.5
4.	Ringworm	4	3.2
5.	Wheezing/bronchitis	11	8.1
6.	Indigestion	8	6.5
7.	Ulcer	12	9.7
8.	Rheumatic problem	8	6.7
9.	Any other disease	10	8.1
10.	No disease	29	23.3
	Total	**124**	**100**

Source: Primary data.

Table 3.17: Details of Insurance Coverage of Domestic Workers

Sl. No	*Insurance coverage*	*No. of domestic workers*	*Percentage*
1.	Covered	5	4.0
2.	Not covered	119	96.0
	Total	**124**	**100**

Source: Primary data.

It is clear from the study (Table 3.17) that 96 per cent of the domestic workers are not covered by insurance and only 4 per cent workers are covered by it. The basic reason is that the worker could not afford to take insurance policy. Secondly they are least interested in insurance because death seems to be a distant phenomenon for them. Instead they are worried about solving their immediate and day-to-day problems. Some of them have invested a small portion of their income in the institutions/places mentioned in Table 3.18.

Table 3.18: Institution/Place Chosen by the Domestic Workers for Savings

Sl. No.	*Preferred Institution*	*No. of domestic workers*	*Percentage*
1.	Bank	17	13.7
2.	Post office	16	12.9
3.	Chit Fund	36	29.0
4.	Employer	16	12.9
5.	No savings	39	31.5
	Total	**124**	**100**

Source: Primary data.

As far as the domestic workers are concerned, the access to formal institutions of savings such as banks and post offices is generally very low. Majority of the domestic workers (29%) save money through private Chit Funds, 13.7 per cent through Banks, 12.9 per cent through Post Office, 12.9 per cent save through their employers and 31.5 per cent have no savings at all. Some of the workers have borrowed huge amount from moneylenders and strive hard to repay the amount from their monthly income. Hence savings seems to be a dream for them.

PROBLEMS OF WOMEN DOMESTIC WORKERS

Lack of Job Security

Lack of job security is a major problem for 8.9 per cent of the domestic workers (Table 3.19). The workers could not entirely rely on their monthly income. They fear that they would be terminated at any time without notice. Only those workers who have a long service under one or two employers and who had gained the trust of their employer are relieved from their problem.

Sexual Exploitation

The principal causes for the sexual exploitation of women domestic workers were acute poverty, lack of employment, unorganized labourforce and lack of community support. Besides, the domestic workers borrow money from their employers in times of dire need. The employers take it as an advantage and sexually exploit them. Hence, 7.3 per cent of the workers stated that sexual exploitation is their chief problem (Table 3.19).

Abuse

This is a very common problem faced by the domestic workers. In this study, 13.7 per cent (Table 3.19) domestic workers consider Abuse as an acute problem. They stated that their employers use filthy languages, harsh words, constant threats and insults without any reason. An innocent worker lamented that her employer often gets irritated whenever she is neatly dressed. She added that her employer never allows her to take rest. A remarkable point is that women employers are more cruel towards women domestic workers. Besides, some of them complained that their employers scold them in English and call them using bad words. In fact, most of them do not know that they could approach the legal professionals and police personnel for redressing their grievances.

Poor Wages

The domestic workers in Tirunelveli city are paid very low wages. According to the study, poor wage is the basic problem for 29 per cent of the domestic workers (Table 3.19). The employers often cheat them by not giving the promised wages. Some of them stated that their employers frequently go for tour and deduct the wages proportionately for the leave days. Hence the workers could not depend on their income.

Heavy Workload

Heavy workload seems to be a major problem for 11.3 per cent of the domestic workers. The domestic workers stated that their employers do not have humanitarian concern on them. They felt that they were treated just like a commodity. Especially when a guest arrives, their workload becomes heavy and the employers seldom pay any extra amount. Instead they are given extra food and some old clothes.

Long Duration of Work

Long duration of work is a crucial problem for 6.5 per cent of the domestic workers (Table 3.19). Especially full time workers have no stipulated working hours. Irrespective of day or night, they have to discharge any type of work assigned to them. In fact, long duration of work spoils the health of the workers. One of the workers commented that her children or husband are not permitted to meet her at the employer's residence during working hours. This in turn affects the family well-being of the workers.

Occupational Disease

Occupational disease seems to be a great threat for 9.7 per cent of the domestic workers. One of the domestic workers stated that her employer frequently asks her to burn several heaps of papers and plastic covers. Another worker stated that her employer gives several buckets of clothes for washing (per day). The inhuman activities of the employers are the basic reasons for the occupation diseases of domestic workers.

Lack of Leave Facility

Leave facility is very essential for the women domestic workers. Especially maternity leave is inevitable. But the employers hesitate to grant even maternity leave to the workers. Sometimes the workers are terminated even if they take leave for genuine reasons. Besides whenever the workers return after taking casual leave, the employers accumulate as many tasks as possible and assign them. The women domestic workers, who were already poor and weak, get psychologically affected. Hence, lack of leave facility is the biggest problem for 4 per cent of the domestic workers (See Table 3.19).

No Retirement Benefits

Even after putting up long years of service, the domestic workers do not get any retirement benefits. In fact, most of them are not aware of such benefits. They simply expect a better wage from their employers so as to satisfy their immediate wants and needs. Hardly 3.2 per cent of the workers are very specific that they should be entitled to retirement benefits like that of organized workers.

Lack of Medical Facility

The domestic workers pay the medical expenses (if any) from their own pockets. Only a few employers reimburse such expenses. Though some of them get treatments in Government hospital at Tirunelveli, they are not satisfied. In case of life threatening diseases, the workers borrow money from moneylenders or relatives or friends to get treated in private Hospital. Huge debt accumulates before they recovered from the disease. As such, lack of medical facility seems to be a great problem for 1.6 per cent of the domestic workers (See Table 3.19).

Charges of Theft

The 4.8 per cent domestic workers stated that they are always suspected for the valuable things or cash missing in the employer's house (Table 3.19). Even trustworthy workers are sometimes charged as thieves. In this context, if the innocent workers take leave, then the employers confirm that they have really stolen and start torturing them in different ways. Some time they are taken to the Police Station and blamed as culprits.

Table 3.19: Problems of Women Domestic Workers

Sl. No.	*Problems*	*No. of domestic workers*	*Percentage*
1.	Lack of job security	11	8.9
2.	Sexual exploitation	9	7.3
3.	Abuse	17	13.7
4.	Poor wages	36	29.0
5.	Heavy workload	14	11.3
6.	Long duration of work	8	6.5
7.	Occupational disease	12	9.7
8.	Lack of leave facility	5	4.0
9.	No retirement benefit	4	3.2
10.	Lack of medical facility	2	1.6
11.	Charges of theft	6	4.8
	Total	**124**	**100**

Source: Primary data.

The study shows that 15.3 per cent of the domestic workers are highly satisfied with domestic work, 25.8 per cent workers are satisfied and the remaining 58.9 per cent workers are not satisfied. Some of them stated that their neighbours and relatives always suspect them as immoral. Besides they felt that their employers never appreciate them. Instead, they always find fault with them. Hence, they are not satisfied with domestic work. But some of them are highly satisfied. They stated that their employers are kind, generous and broadminded (Table 3.20).

Table 3.20: Job Satisfaction of the Domestic Workers

Sl. No.	*Opinion*	*No. of domestic workers*	*Percentage*
1.	Highly satisfied	19	15.3
2.	Satisfied	32	25.8
3.	Not satisfied	73	58.9
	Total	**124**	**100**

Source: Primary data.

Findings

- The study shows that 84.7 per cent of the women domestic workers serve on full time basis and 15.3 per cent workers serve on part time basis.
- Majority of the domestic workers (33.1%) are serving three employers.
- It was found out that most of the domestic workers work for 6 to 8 hours per day.
- There is no agreement between the employer and the domestic workers. Hence the domestic workers are frequently exploited by their employers.
- As for as Tirunelveli city is concerned, there is lack of improvement in the wages of domestic workers. If the workers demand for more wages, the employers simply terminate them and look out for new workers.
- The domestic workers have no legal status. There is no scheme or legal provisions in force to regulate the

employment of domestic workers. Hence, they are cheated by the employers by levying overwork than what is actually agreed upon (orally). Besides under-payment and non-payment of wages are also faced by the workers.

- Majority of the domestic workers in Tirunelveli city belong to the age group of 20 to 40 years.
- The study shows that most of the domestic workers are educated below SSLC level. Some of them are illiterates and are too innocent to understand the behaviour of the employers. But the workers are keenly interested in educating their children. Hence their status in the society would be raised at a rapid rate.
- It was found out that 81.5 per cent of the women domestic workers are married. Most of them have 1 to 2 children in their families.
- Majority of the domestic workers (44.4%) have 2 to 4 members in their families.
- The women domestic workers have taken up domestic work mainly due to economic reasons. They toil to free them from the clutches of moneylenders, unable to repay the long existing debts.
- It is clear from the study that most of the domestic workers (58.1%) have 2 earning members in their families.
- The personal income of most of the domestic workers ranges from Rupees 1000 to Rupees 1500 per month. The workers, who are single earners, find it difficult to manage their family with the poor income. But the family income of the most of the workers ranges from Rupees 3000 to Rupees 4500.
- The study shows that 91.1 per cent of domestic workers live in rented houses.
- The domestic workers spend a huge portion of their income on rent and grocery.
- The domestic workers suffer from various occupational diseases like ulcer, wheezing, back pain, leg pain, body pain etc.

- Majority of the domestic workers (96%) do not have insurance coverage. This is mainly because of the fact that they could not afford to pay the premiums. Some of them are ignorant of the benefits of insurance.
- It was found out that majority of the domestic workers (29%) prefer to save their money in private Chit Fund agencies.
- The domestic workers in Tirunelveli city are not recognized as workers. They have no right to worker's compensation, weekly holidays and minimum wages.
- The low social and economic status of the occupation adversely affects the marital prospects of women domestic workers. Their marriage proposal often gets cancelled due to the fact that they are not recognized as labourers. Instead they are often suspected to be immoral and indecent.
- The full time women domestic workers are more subject to sexual exploitation than the part time workers.
- The domestic workers get medical treatment from Government Hospital situated at High Grounds, Tirunelveli. But they complained that they do not get proper treatment in the Government Hospital. Most of them could not afford to get treated in private hospitals. Only a few could afford.
- Besides wages, the domestic workers are not given any other benefits either by the employer or by the Government to take care of their health, safety and future.
- Domestic workers are not registered and are not shown in employment statistics.

Suggestions

- A separate Act should be passed by the Government of Tamilnadu to regulate the employment of domestic workers.
- The employers should pay at least one month's pay as bonus once in a year. This would help the domestic workers in several ways.
- Regular meals should be given to the domestic workers irrespective of the nature of work performed.

- The domestic workers in Tirunelveli city should create awareness among themselves to form Union so that they could fight for their problems. A membership fee of at least Rupees 10 per year should be fixed for this purpose. A great deal of progress could be achieved through collective action of the Union.
- The organized labour in Tirunelveli city should encourage the unorganized domestic workers to get themselves organized.
- The local Government of Tirunelveli city should compel the domestic workers to wear identity cards stating their name, address, age, name of the employer/employers and other important details regarding their employment.
- While employing domestic workers, the employers should record written agreements stating the nature of domestic work, duration of work and remuneration details.
- Minimum wages of domestic workers should be fixed by the Government on the basis of cost of living index in Tirunelveli city and the employers should be compelled to contribute towards Provident Fund and Gratuity benefits of the workers.
- Maternity leave should be provided to the women domestic workers. If not, the employers should be heavily fined.
- The domestic workers should be given two weeks paid leave (per year) in addition to weekly off. This would enable them to maintain health and take care of their family.
- The domestic workers should compulsorily take insurance policy at least for a small amount. The employers should share the premium amount.
- The minimum age for domestic workers (especially for female workers) should be fixed as thirty. This may avoid frequent incidents of sexual harassments.
- The employers should remit an advance deposit in the bank/ post office in the name of domestic workers while recruiting them. The workers could utilize the amount in times of emergency.

- The employers should give valid reasons for terminating the domestic workers. A reasonable period of notice should be given in the event of termination so that the workers could seek another employment. Sudden termination should necessarily be accompanied by huge and immediate compensation without any excuse.
- The employers should be instructed by the labour office to pay the remuneration of domestic workers through bank or post office.
- Extra payment should be given to the domestic workers while assigning extra work other than what is actually agreed upon. Otherwise the workers would not be sincere in discharging extra work.
- It is of paramount importance to provide annual increment benefits to the domestic workers.
- The brutal activities of the employers towards women domestic workers must be punished instantly without any delay. This may surely avoid the happening of such incidents in the future.

Conclusion

The domestic workers remain the most exploited even after five decades of independence. The contribution of domestic workers to the economy is ignored and deprived of social benefits and workers' rights. Hence, their problems are to be analyzed by the Government in different dimensions. If the domestic workers are given the same status as of regular workers, there will be betterment in their working conditions which in turn would lift their status in the society.

REFERENCES

Boserup, Ester (1970), *Women's Role in Economic Development*, St. Martins Press, New York.

Towards Equality: Report of the Committee on the Status of Women in India, Department of Social Welfare, Ministry of Education and Social Welfare, Government of India (1974) December, New Delhi.

Sinha, G.P Ranade. S.N., (1975) *Women Construction Workers*, Allied Publishers, Mumbai.

ILO (1984) Introduction to Social Security, Geneva, International Labour Office.

Gopalan, Sarala (1995) *Women and Employment in India*, Har Anand Publications, New Delhi.

Occupational Health Issues of Women in the Unorganised Sector (1998), Report of the Task Force on Health, National Commission on Self Employed Women, February.

Yadhav. N. Kashyap, Rani (1998), Working Women and Their Constraints, *Journal of Social Research*, Delhi, Jan-March.

Mittal, L.N (1998), Women the Worse Hit, *Social Welfare*, January.

Nirmala Banerjee (1999), Women is Emerging Labour Market, *Indian Journal of Labour Economics*, Vol. 42, No. 4.

Koli. P.A (2005), *Economic Development and Environment Issues*, Serials Publications, New Delhi.

Nambiar. A.C.K (2005), *Population Development and the Environment*, Serials Publications, New Delhi.

Sujata Gothoskar (2005), New Initiatives in Organising Strategy in the Informal Economy, Case Study of Domestic Workers Organizing in India, Committee for Asian Women, Bangkok.

Debasree Laheri (2007), Abuse of Child Domestic Workers in India: Crises and Challenges, *The Indian Police Journal*, Vol. LIV No. 4, October-December.

South Asia Workshop on Home-based Work, (2007) A Home Net Report, December, Ahmedabad.

www.labourfile.org/newsmore.aspz?Nd=23

www.indiatogether.org/2004/nov/hrt-domhelp.htm

www.globaljusticecenter.org/papers2005/ally_eng.htm

www.kishorecariappa.blogspot.com/2007/09/maids-get their-due.htm

www.teresas.ac.in/main/Domestic%20workers%20meel.asp

http://en.wikipedia.org/wiki/Tirunelveli

www.hindu.com/2007/07/15/stories/2007071554480600.htm

4

Problems Faced by Brick Kiln Workers of Southern Districts of Tamilnadu

Prof. C. Eugine Franco*

Abstract

The Indian brick industry which is the second largest producer in the world, next to China, is one of the largest employment generating industries, employing millions of workers. The Indian brick industry has more than 1 lakh production units producing about 100 billion bricks annually. The industry has an annual turnover of more than Rs. 10,000 crores. Bricks can be manufactured only in places where clay with suitable characteristics is available. Ground-moulded and table-moulded country kiln brick making are labour-intensive and consume more firewood. It is needless to say that brick kiln workers, being unorganized, face a lot of problems such as inadequate wages, lack of job security, excessive hours of work, health hazard, indebtedness and the like. The researcher is interested to study the various problems faced by brick kiln workers of southern districts of Tamilnadu, India. The study covers Melapalayam and

* **SG Lecturer in Commerce, St. Xaviers College (Autonomous), Palayamkottai, Tamilnadu.**

Panakudi areas of Triunelveli district, Eral of Tuticorin and Thovalai of Kanyakumari district.

The study has been undertaken with the following main objectives:

1. To study the demographic characteristics of brick kiln workers;
2. To identify the problems faced by brick kiln workers of the study area;
3. To measure and rank the given problems; and
4. To suggest ways and means for overcoming the problems of brick kiln workers of the study area.

One hundred and fifty respondents (50 from each district) were selected from various brick kilns of the three districts by applying stratified random sampling. The study is based on both primary as well as secondary data. And, the study covers a period of 6 months ranging from September, 2007 to February, 2008. Field work for the study was carried on by the researcher himself. For collecting the primary data from the respondents an interview schedule was structured and used. The interview schedule was administered to the members in the vernacular and the data were recorded by the researcher in the schedule. Garrett ranking technique was applied to rank the problems faced by brick kiln workers by using the following formula:

$$\text{Per cent position} = \frac{100\,(Rij - 0.5)}{Nj}$$

It was found that the first and foremost problem of brick kiln workers of the study area is inadequate wages with the score of 61.19 while the problem of transportation was ranked the last one with the score of 35.95. The only way to put an end to this problem is ensuring minimum wages to the worker of brick kiln.

Introduction

In India, clay bricks have been extensively used for centuries and are the predominant construction material. The conventional practice of firing clay bricks in traditional kilns consumes large quantities of coal, firewood, and other biomass fuels. The Indian brick industry which is the second largest producer in the world, next to China, consumes more than 24 million tons of coal annually. Brick making is a traditional unorganized industry, generally confined to rural and semi-urban areas. It is one of the largest employment generating industries, employing millions of workers. The Indian brick industry has more than 1 lakh production units producing about 100 billion bricks annually. The industry has an annual turnover of more than Rs. 10,000 crores.

Demographic Characteristics of Brick Kiln Workers

Table 4.1: Age-wise Classification of the Respondents

Age	*No. of respondents*	*Percentage*
Up to 25	47	31.33
26-35	45	30
36-45	35	23.33
Above 45	23	15.34
Total	**150**	**100**

Source: Primary data.

Table 4.1 reveals the age group of the respondents. It is clear from the table that the number of youngsters (up to 25), and young adults (26-35) who are at brick industry is higher (61.33%) than that of full adults and the lower old age (above 45).

Table 4.2: Sex-wise Classification of Respondents

Sex	*No. of respondents*	*Percentage*
Male	91	60.67
Female	59	39.33
Total	**150**	**100**

Source: Primary data.

Table 4.2 shows that the number of male workers of brick kiln is larger (60.67%) than that of the number of female brick kiln workers.

Table 4.3: Education-wise Classification of Respondents

Educational status	*No. of respondents*	*Percentage*
No formal education	18	12
Primary education	60	40
Middle school	52	34.67
High school	18	12
Higher secondary	2	1.33
Total	**150**	**100**

Source: Primary data.

It is evident from Table 4.3 that majority of the respondents (40%) have only primary education. It is significant to note that 18 have no formal education and 52 have middle school education only. Thus, it is clear that the educational status of the most of the respondents is very poor.

Table 4.4: Distribution of Respondents on the Basis of Marital Status

Marital status	*No. of the respondents*	*Percentage*
Married	105	70
Unmarried	45	30
Total	**150**	**100**

Source: Primary data.

It is evident from the Table 4.4 that most of the respondents (70%) are married.

Table 4.5: Income-wise Classification of Respondents

Monthly income	*No. of respondents*	*Percentages*
Below Rs. 500	Nil	Nil
Rs. 501-Rs. 1500	47	31.33
Rs. 1501-Rs. 2500	73	48.87
Above Rs. 2500	30	20
Total	**150**	**100**

Source: Primary data.

It is clear that most of the respondents' (80%) monthly income is just up to Rs. 2500.

Problems of Brick Kiln Workers

The following ten problems have been identified: no job guarantee, inadequate wages, inadequate working conditions, bondage, excessive hours of work, excessive physical work, physical and health hazard, breathing problem, indebtedness and transportation problem.

For rating the problems faced by brick kiln workers Garrett ranking technique was applied and accordingly the following formula was used:

$$\text{Per cent position} = \frac{100\,(Rij - 0.5)}{Nj}$$

where,

Rij = rank given for the ith variable by the *j*th respondent.

Nj = number of variables ranked by the *j*th respondent.

MASTER TABLE SHOWING THE PROBLEMS OF BRICK KILN WORKERS AND THER RANKINGS

Rank	*JS*	*IW*	*IWC*	*B*	*EHW*	*EPW*	*HH*	*BP*	*ID*	*TP*	*Total*
1.	43	26	20	7	12	19	3	2	17	1	150
2.	21	43	12	3	16	16	13	8	14	4	150
3.	9	18	12	3	14	22	18	10	37	7	150
4.	9	16	15	5	16	21	28	14	16	10	150
5.	8	10	12	8	18	11	25	29	18	11	150
6.	12	165	8	11	22	12	29	24	8	8	150
7.	14	7	12	17	18	23	13	22	10	14	150
8.	12	7	35	26	11	10	9	12	5	23	150
9.	13	3	16	44	8	6	7	15	9	29	150
10.	9	4	8	26	15	10	5	14	16	43	150
Total	**150**	**150**	**150**	**150**	**150**	**150**	**150**	**150**	**150**	**150**	**150**

Job Security

Job security is the measure of job-loss risk an individual has in his or her job. A job that offers high level of job security indicates that a person in such a job would have a small chance of becoming unemployed whereas a job with low job security suggests that a person in such a job has a high probability of becoming unemployed. Typically, government jobs are considered very secure while private sector jobs, especially unorganized sector jobs, are generally believed to offer lower job security.

JOB SECURITY

X	*JS (F)*	*FX*
81	43	3483
70	21	1470
63	9	567
58	9	522
52	8	416
48	12	576
42	14	588
37	12	444
29	13	377
18	9	162
Total	**150**	**8605**

Mean = 57.37

Indebtedness

It is well-known that the Indian worker, both industrial and agricultural, is born in debt, continuous to live in debt and dies in debt. Most of the brick kiln workers have debts passed on to their shoulders from their parents who themselves inherit it from their parents. Among economic causes of indebtedness inadequate wages take the first place. For the indebtedness of the workers, workers' personal habits also contribute a lot.

INDEBTEDNESS

X	ID(F)	FX
81	17	1377
70	14	980
63	37	2331
58	16	928
52	18	936
48	8	384
42	10	420
37	5	185
29	9	261
18	16	288
Total	**150**	**8090**

Mean = 53.93

Health Hazards

The conventional practice of firing clay bricks in Bull's Trench Kilns (BTK) and rural country clamps consumes huge quantities of energy in terms of coal, firewood and other fuels. They are also notorious as highly polluting establishments, affecting not just the flora and fauna, but also posing severe threats to human health.

HEALTH HAZARDS

X	HH(F)	FX
81	3	243
70	13	910
63	18	1134
58	28	1624
52	25	1300
48	29	1392
42	13	546
37	09	333
29	07	203
18	05	90
Total	**150**	**7775**

Mean = 51.83

Excessive Physical Work

By the passage of time physical fitness begins to decrease and may impair work capacity particularly in physically demanding blue-collar jobs. Physical work load should be adjusted according to the work capacity of each individual worker for preventing overstrains, fatigue, disorders and injuries.

EXCESSIVE PHYSICAL WORK

X	*EPW(F)*	*FX*
81	19	1539
70	16	1120
63	22	1386
58	21	1218
52	11	572
48	12	576
42	23	966
37	10	370
29	06	174
18	10	180
Total	**150**	**8101**

Mean = 54.01

Inadequate Wages

One of the severe problems that is being faced by the workers of unorganized sector is that they are not given wages what they deserve. It is needless to say that there are no stipulations and regulations over payment of wages to brick kiln workers. As a result, the wages that is given to the workers of brick kiln becomes unfair and inadequate.

INADEQUATE WAGES

X	IW(F)	FX
81	26	2106
70	43	3010
63	18	1134
58	16	928
52	10	520
48	16	768
42	7	294
37	7	259
29	3	87
18	4	72
Total	**150**	**9178**

Mean = 61.19

Excessive Hours of Work

According to the unorganized sector workers' Bill, 2002, the working hours are defined as 9 hours a day. It further says that every worker shall be entitled a weekly holiday, causal or sick leave and 15 days earned leave in a year. However, in most of the brick kilns the workers are to work for more hours for both Pull and Push forces.

EXCESSIVE HOURS OF WORK

X	EHW(F)	FX
81	12	972
70	16	1120
63	14	882
58	16	928
52	18	936
48	22	1056
42	18	756
37	11	407
29	08	232
18	15	217
Total	**150**	**7559**

Mean = 50.39

Inadequate Working Conditions

Assurance of adequate and safe working conditions is of paramount importance in brick kiln industries. A resent study conducted by the Pasumai Trust, Tiruvallur, and the People's Forum for Human Rights, Chennai has established that prolonged exposure to sand, dust and heat of kilns led to workers developing dermatological and gastroenterological problems.

INADEQUATE WORKING CONDITION

X	*IWC(F)*	*FX*
81	20	1620
70	12	840
63	12	756
58	15	870
52	12	624
48	087	384
42	12	504
37	35	1295
29	16	464
18	08	144
Total	**150**	**7501**

Mean = 50.01

Breathing Problem

The very nature of environment and surrounding of a brick kiln industry leads to a lot of physical problems such as wheezing, asthma and breathing. It is well known that breathing problem gradually develops illness like wheezing, asthma and the like.

BREATHING PROBLEM

X	BP(F)	FX
81	02	162
70	08	560
63	10	630
58	14	812
52	29	1508
48	24	1152
42	22	924
37	12	444
29	15	435
18	14	252
Total	**150**	**6879**

Mean = 45.86

Bondage

Peoples' Vigilance Committee on Human Rights, (PVCHR) has come to know of the existence of a large number of bonded labourers along with their wives and children being held in bondage by a brick kiln owner and subjected to inhuman beatings, torture, and death threats when they ask for their wages in a village in West Bengal.

BONDAGE

	X	B(F)	FX
	81	07	567
	70	03	210
	63	03	189
	58	05	290
	52	08	416
	48	11	528
	42	17	714
	37	26	962
	29	44	1276
	18	26	468
	Total	**150**	**5620**

Mean = 37.47

Transportation Problem

Transportation becomes a problem for all those workers who have to commute every day from their far away dwelling places to their brick kiln industries. The problem becomes more aggressive when they have no or low access to public transportation and when they have no private or own transportation facility at their disposal.

TRANSPORTATION PROBLEM

X	*TP(F)*	*FX*
81	1	81
70	4	280
63	7	441
58	10	580
52	11	572
48	8	384
42	14	588
37	23	851
29	29	841
18	43	774
Total	**150**	**5392**

Mean = 35.95

Findings

It was found that the first and foremost problem of brick kiln workers in the study area is inadequate wages with the Garrett Mean score of 61.19. And, the second rank goes to the problem of no job security with the score of 57.37. Excessive physical work has been ranked as the third problem of brick kiln workers with the score of 54.01. Brick kiln workers' indebtedness was given fourth rank with the score of 53.93. The problem of health hazard comes as the fifth one with 51.83 score. An excessive hour of work was ranked sixth with the score of 50.39. The problem of inadequate working condition was considered as the next important problem of brick kiln workers with the score of 50.01. Breathing problem caused by brick kiln industry was identified as the eighth important problem with the score of 45.86. Ninth rank goes to bondage with a score of 37.47 and the last rank goes to the problem concerning transportation with the Garrett Mean score of 35.95.

FINDINGS

Rank	*Problem*	*Score*
I	Inadequate wages	61.19
II	No Job Security	57.37
III	Excessive physical work	54.01
IV	Indebtedness	53.93
V	Health hazards	51.83
VI	Excessive hours of work	50.39
VII	Inadequate working conditions	50.01
VIII	Breathing problem	45.86
IX	Bondage	37.47
X	Transportation problem	35.95

REFERENCES

L. Mishra, *Unorganized Labour-deprivation and Emancipation*, Manak Publications Pvt. Limited. 1999.

M.V. Moorthy, *Principles of Labour Welfare* Ed. 2, Oxford and IBH Publishing Company 1982.

Oxford Children's Encyclopedia, Oxford University Press, 1991.

www. wikipedia.org.

The Hindu, Dated Sep. 7th, 2006.

Hindu News Update Service, July 28th, 2006.

5

Plight of Agricultural Labour

Prof. S. Gurusamy*

India lives in village as stated by Mahatma Gandhi. About 70 per cent of our people are engaged in agricultural and related activities. Agricultural and allied activities workers are almost unorganized.

Especially rural female workers are performing both in household and agricultural activities. The poor in India are overwhelmingly concentrated in rural areas, engaged in agricultural and non-agricultural occupations. They are mainly labour households, basically comprising of wage labourers as well as self-employed petty cultivators who are peasants and workers. They constitute the most backward, unorganized and deprived section of the workforce in rural India. Rural labourers as a whole a depressed group some of them are even more vulnerable as bonded labourer are the most exploited group living in precarious conditions.

Rural labour comprises both agricultural labour and other engaged in non-agricultural manual work in rural areas. According to 2001 census, out of 341 million total workers constituting 40.64 per cent of the total population, 79.18 per cent resided in rural areas.

* **Professor and Head, Department of Sociology, Gandhigram Rural University, Gandhigram – 624 302, Dindigul, Tamilnadu.**

In 2001 the proportion of agricultural labourers per hundred cultivatiors was 67 as against 60 in 1981. Females constituted 39.12 per cent of the total agricultural labourers in 2001 and their growth rate during 1991-2001 was higher (39.91%) as compared to the male labourers (36.92%).

The National Commission on Rural Labour (NCRL), constituted by the Government of India in its report submitted in 1991, defined the rural labourer: "A person who is living and working in rural area had engaged in agricultural and/or non-agricultural activities requiring physical labour and getting wages or remuneration partially or wholly in cash or kind or both during the year or such own-account workers like small farmers and artisans who are not usually hiring in labourers but are a part of the petty production in rural areas" (GOI, 1991 P A – 3).

The package of various labour laws has not benefited them in many crucial areas specially wages, health, maternity and social security. Government institutions and the empowerment machinery have failed to provide awareness of their political, legal and natural rights and hence they continue to live in drudgery.

India is a country of villages, about 75 per cent of the people are living in rural areas. There are about six lakh villages in which more than 70 per cent of the people directly depend on agriculture for earning their livelihood. Agriculture plays a predominant role in our national income. India has attained self-sufficiency in food production after 60 years of Independence. The credit for this, no doubt, goes to agricultural workers who spend most of their time in slush and mud but with half-appeased appetite. The needs of the urban people are not satisfied without the help of rural farm workers. These labourers devote their life on land for raising the crops.

Even though the agricultural labourers are hard workers, they face various problems throughout their life. Their earning is a very low, and their employment avenue also is very limited. In a monsoon country like India, crop cultivation entirely depends on rainfall. If there is heavy rain everything in the life of the rural labourers will be affected to a large extent. The agricultural labourers do not have any guarantee for their full employment on the land. They have employment opportunities only during season and during off-season, they have to face the problem of unemployment and under-employment. Poverty and indebtedness are the common features of Indian agricultural labourers. Problems of child labour, bonded labour, wage disparity among male and female are also found every where. Most of the time, the agricultural labourers are forced to go out of their village in search of employment opportunities.

After the attainment of freedom, our Government has realized that the development of the country has no meaning without the development of the poor segments, particularly the development of the agricultural labourers. Through various Five Year Plans our Government has introduced several programmes for the improvement of the lot of this sector. One of the major objectives of the Rural Development Programme is 'to bridge the gap between various non-agricultural employment opportunities in the villages with the help of local resources.

Agricultural Labour: The Scenario

It is rather difficult to define the term 'Agricultural Labour' in precise terms. However, it will be useful to refer to some of the attempts made by experts in this connection. The First Agricultural Labour Enquiry Committee (1950-51) enlarged the definition of agricultural labour to include 'those who are engaged in other agricultural occupations like dairy farming, horticulture, raising of livestock, bees, poultry etc.'

In the context of Indian conditions, the definition is not adequate because it is not possible to completely separate those working for wages from others. There are people who do not work throughout the year but only during a part of it. Therefore, the First Agricultural Labour Enquiry Committee (A.L.E.C) used the concepts of 'Agricultural Labour Household'. If half or more members of a household have wage employment in agriculture, that household should be termed as 'Agricultural Labour Household'. The Second Agricultural Labour Enquiry Committee substituted income criteria and said that an agricultural labour household is one whose main source of income is wage from agriculture.

According to the National Commission of Labour, an agricultural labourer is one who is basically unskilled and unorganized and has little for his livelihood other than personal labour'. Thus, persons whose main source of income is wage employment fall in this category.

Permanent or attached labourers generally work on annual or seasonal basis and they work in some sort of contract. Their wages are determined by custom and tradition. On the other hand, temporary and they are paid at the market rate.

Under the second group come small farmers who possess very little land and, therefore, have to devote most of their time working in the lands of others as labourers. Sharecroppers are those who, while sharing the produce of the land for their work, also work as labourers. Tenants are those who not only work on the leased land but also work as agricultural labourers.

Working Condition of Agricultural Labourers

Agricultural work is laborious in nature unlike industrial work. The agricultural labourers have to toil in the hot sun and intermittent rainfall. Their rest interval is very limited. Due to labour force, they have only limited employment opportunities.

Working Condition of Attached Labour

Though we have Constitutional backing for abolition of bonded labour system, still we have bonded labour force where the availability of opening is limited. They are exploited by their land-owners all through their life. They are not compelled to work in the farms of the land-owners but also in their houses.

Extent of Employment

The employment of agricultural labourer may be either seasonal or casual. Casual workers are employed during peak agricultural seasons, while seasonal workers attend to routine operation all the year.

On an average, the adult male agricultural labourers are employed for 189 days in a year and the women workers are employed 134 days in a year. The casual workers are to find employment on an average of 200 days whereas attached workers are employed for 326 days in a year. Hours of work in agriculture have been found to be unduly long, particularly during the peak agricultural seasons. During harvesting and threshing, casual workers work about 10 to 11 hours a day without suitable rest intervals, and at other periods they are exposed to comparatively short rest intervals, during the other periods they work under scorching sunlight. In fact, there is no regularity in hours of work which depend on the good will and cooperation between the workers and employers and on local customs.

Income and Wage

Even though the agricultural labourers are engaged longer hours in the field, the wage given to them is not equal to their hard work. For a long period, they have been demanding higher wages. The Communist Party and other political parties helped farm workers to get higher wages. They are paid in the form of cash or kind. The income of agricultural labourers is very low. Their wage structure is between Rs. 10.00 and 20.00 to 35.00 per day for the males, depending upon the nature of work and distance of workplace.

Living Condition of Agricultural Labourers

In the status hierarchy, the agricultural labourers are indentified as the lowers rung of the social ladder. In social stratification, almost all agricultural labourers are from lower caste or schedule caste, tribals and other backward communities. Due to untouchability, low income and other superstitious beliefs the agricultural labour is poorly placed in the status hierarchy.

It is clear that the economic living and social life of agricultural labourers are very deplorable. They are also poor that they have to fall in debt for physical existence. Poverty and indebtedness make them work as bonded labourers and live as serfs. In many cases indebtedness persists for generations and long with it exists serfdom.

Our Governments both State and Central are concerned about the problems of agricultural labourers and have given special consideration to agricultural labourers.

Programmes Launched by the Government

With a view to improve the condition of agricultural labour various programmes are launched by the Governments in India.

Such programmes are target group oriented; the State governments have taken up programmes in collaboration with Central Government and launched specific programmes to meet the employment needs of this depressed section.

Suggestions for the Improvement of Agricultural Labour

1. To ensure full employment to the agricultural labourers in the village the Government must come forward with certain job-oriented and technical skill programmes particularly in the Khadi, cottage and village industrial sectors to generate local self-employment amongst agricultural labourers in the village.
2. Since Agricultural labourers are unaware of various social welfare legislations and provisions available to various social divisions, the voluntary agencies may, in collaboration with governments, give wide publicity through community organization particularly in the Minimum Wage Act which should be effectively implemented.
3. Except in peak periods there is no employment opportunity. At that time the Government must come forward with employment opportunities like road repairing, deepening of ponds and wells etc.
4. The Government must include some more agro-based works also in the Minimum Wage Act. This would enlarge the scope of work performance in allied sectors by agricultural labour in village.
5. Co-option of agricultural labour in the local self-governing institutions must be ensured in order to provide representation to this section.
6. Land Reforms Act must be strictly enforced by the Government and surplus lands must be distributed among landless agricultural labourers.
7. In the National Commission on Labour, representation to agricultural labourers must be provided so that their economic interest be protected.

8. The workers have to work for very long hours. This needs to be regulated and not to exceed 8 hours per day. Government must take some sincere attempts to regulate working hours of the agricultural labourers in rural areas.

9. As agricultural labourers are harassed and exploited by employers they are unable to develop individuality, originality and independence. The provision of 10 hours work for males and 8 hours work for females must strictly be enforced. Organization of agricultural labour also pave the way for the realization of this object.

10. Since agricultural labourers are unaware of various social welfare legislations and provisions available to them, the voluntary agencies may, in collaboration with Governments, give wide publicity through community organizations particularly about the Minimum Wage Act, Target Group Programmes, Employment Guarantee Schemes, Insurance Schemes, Social Welfare Measures etc.

11. Policies and programmes need to facilitate labour access to health, education, nutrition, skill, capacity building for income generation with a focus on rural labour.

REFERENCES

1. Agrawal, A.N. *Indian Economy—Problems of Development and Planning,* Vishwa Prakashan, New Delhi, (1995).
2. Alexander, K.C. *Peasant Organisations in South India,* National Institute of Rural Development, Hydrabad, (1983).
3. Datt, R. et al. *Indian Economy,* S.Chand and Company Ltd., New Delhi, (1996).
4. Mhople, P.R. et al. "Socio-economic Dimensions of Farm Women Labour", *Rural India,* (1998), pp.192-195 (September to October).
5. Ruplekha, Borah, "Perceived Drudgery and Factors Influencing Time Spent in Agricultural Operations by Farm Women", *Rural India,* (1998), pp. 214-221 (November).
6. Sharma, Gurpree, "Labour Force Participation and Agricultural Wages in India", *Rural India,* (1998), pp. 128-136, (June).
7. Radhakrishna (Ed), Empowering Rural Labour in India, New Delhi, Institute of Human Development, (1998).

6

Women Labourers in Unorganised Sector

Dr. S. Maria John*
Dr. Mrs. A. Mary Grace**

Abstract

India has all along followed a proactive policy in the matter of Labour policy in India has evolved in response to specific needs of the situation to suit requirements of planned economic development and social justice and has a two-fold objective namely maintaining industrial peace and promoting the welfare of labour. The unorganized sector of the economy is primarily labour intensive but less rewarding to the workers in compensation to their efforts put in production. The characteristics of the unorganized labour are specified by the Second Commission on Labour (2002) as self employed persons involved in jobs, agriculture workers, migrant labours, casual and

* M.Com. M.B.A., B.Ed. PGDCA. Ph.D., Reader and Research Advisor, Department of Commerce, Cardamom Planters' Association College, (Affiliated to Madurai Kamaraj University), Bodinayakanur – 625 513, Tamilnadu.

** M.A., M.Phil., Ph.D., S.G. Lecturer in History, J.A. College for Women (Autonomous), Mother Teresa Women's University, Periyakulam – 625 601, Theni District.

contract workers and home-based artisans. The nature of the employment relationship is the key determinant factor of unorganized labour.

The unorganised labour accounted for more than per cent of the total workforce according to census 2001. The majority of women workers come under this category and is employed in the rural areas. Among the rural women workers, 87 per cent are employed in agriculture as labourers and cultivators. In the urban areas, 80 per cent of the women workers are employed in household industries, petty traders, domestic servants and workers in the cottage industries. Though women constitute a significant part of workforce, they lag behind men and they are the neglected section of the society. Moreover, it is an established fact that women bear a disproportionately heavy burden of work than men as they have to contribute more time in the care economy that is the domestic work.

Problems and Women Workers

It is a recognized fact that there is still no society in the world in which women workers enjoy the same opportunities as men. The women unorganized sector are facing so many problems. According to the 2001 census about 96 per cent of women workers in India are in the unorganized sector. The rise of female participating in unorganized sector is due to the compulsion and employer's preference for female employee. Their ignorance, illiteracy and poverty have added fuel to their woes all the more. Women are considered the human resource of choice for the unorganized sector because they lack education and training and are amenable to accept lower wages for equal work due to gender casting. On the basis of Government reports the major problems faced by women are:

1. Women have to work under very poor working and living conditions.
2. Women workers are paid lower and marginal wages.
3. They have to work for long hours even forced to work in late night without protection.
4. They suffer from job insecurity and under-employment.

5. They are deprived of adequate social security, safety and welfare provisions.
6. They are not protected by any government labour organizations.
7. They have to face sexual harassment at the workplace.
8. They have lack of outside linkages and opportunities.
9. There is no job security.

The various problems faced by the workers and identified for the purpose of the study were categorized as problems relating to:

1. Working Conditions
2. Living Conditions
3. Time of Work
4. Remuneration
5. Security
6. Harassment
7. Protection of Rights

Steps to be Taken

The empowerment of women is an important necessity of the present day. The efforts of the government to improve the conditions of the women workers are praiseworthy. But due to the corrupt practices of the functionaries the beneficiaries are not capable to utilize these programmes. The efforts of the government proved to be failure. In order to improve the conditions of unorganized women workers some of the suggestions are recommended:

- Women workers should be educated and make them aware about their rights and legislative provisions.
- Effective steps should be taken to reflect the duty of the government and society to protect the Human Rights of Women workers.

- The legislations, which prevent all forms of discriminations and guarantee equal job opportunities, should be strictly enacted and implemented.
- To protect the human rights of unorganized women workers, necessary amendments are required to be made in the labour laws.
- For the payment of compensation in case of injury or exploitation in unorganized sector a Compensation Board to be formed.
- Women must be motivated to utilize the existing programmes.
- To fight against the discriminations and exploitation, the women workers must be encouraged to form groups.
- Conduct Human Rights educating camps at regular intervals and strengthen the Human Rights Commission to protect the vulnerable section of women workers.
- There should be a proper regulation of unorganized sector industries, which will assume women workers job security, healthy work environment at least minimum wages, maternity and child care benefits.
- Women worker leaders must be included in the policy formulation and other decision-making processes relating to the welfare of the women workers.
- The political will of the government, financial resources and self-confidence of the women workers only lead to the improvement of their condition, not only women but men also hence to chance their attitudes towards for their betterment.

The unorganized sector has been more vulnerable and ignored sector in India. It holds an important place in Indian economy. So the unorganized women workers' development should the viewed as an issue in social development to be seen as an essential component in every dimension of development. In order to get empowerment the government and the social workers may contribute significant role in making women workers capable, self-reliant and well organized. It is worthwhile to create the awakening among unorganized women so that they can come up by taking care of themselves. Thus, there is no exaggeration in saying that the backbone of Indian workforce is the unorganized sector. Yet there is a tendency to ignore this mass of workforce as these millions who belong to unorganized sector are politically powerless and economically weak. So, there is an urgent need to give top priority to the issues and problems of the workers of unorganized sector.

Labour is a service performed by workers for wages as distinguished from rendered entrepreneurs for profits. It is also meant as an economic group comprising those who do manual labour or work for wages. Labour as a policy in India, has evolved in response to specific needs of the situation to suit requirements of planned economic development and social justice and has objectives of maintaining industrial peace promoting the welfare of labour reforms.

The Government of India is committed to the task of carrying forward the process of labour reforms which is an integral part of the Government's economic policy. In order to meet certain immediate needs, the government initiated steps to carry out amendments in some important labour laws to make them contemporary to the changing needs of the time. Accordingly amendments were carried on in the Trade Unions Act, 1926; Industrial Disputes Act, 1947; Payment of Wages Act, 1936; Factories Act, 1948; Employees Provident Act, 1965 and Child Labour Act, 1986.

India has all along followed a proactive policy in the matter of Labour policy which India has evolved in response to specific needs of the situation to suit requirements of planned economic development and social justice and has a two-fold objective namely maintaining industrial peace and promoting the welfare of labour.

Workers who have not been able to organize themselves in pursuit of their common interest due to certain constraints like casual nature of employment, ignorance and illiteracy are termed as unorganized sector. According to the Central Statistical

Organization, "The unorganized sector includes all those unincorporated enterprises, the household industries which are not regulated by any legislation and which do not maintain annual accounts or balance sheet." The unorganized sector of the economy is primarily labour-intensive but less rewarding to the workers in compensation to their efforts put in production. The characteristics of the unorganized labour are specified by the Second Commission on Labour (2002) as self-employed persons involved in jobs, agriculture workers, migrant labourers, casual and contract workers and home-based artisans. The nature of the employment relationship is the key determinant factor of unorganized labour.

The various types of labourers under unorganized sector included, Handloom and Silk Weaving (HHSW), Tree climbers (TREE), Loading and unloading porters of public sector vehicles (LULT), Scavengers (STVE), Tailors (TAIL), Auto and Taxi drivers (AUTO), Hair dressers and Beauticians in parlours (HRBP), Cooks (COOK), Porters in shops and business concerns (LULC), Domestic servants (DOME), Cobblers (FLGM), Bullock holders (BKCO), House makers with palm leaves (PALC), Plastic basket makers (PLIO), Agarbatti makers (INCS), Copara workers (COPL), Bicycle repairers (CYRE), Engineers (ENGR), Fast Food caterers (CATR), Shopkeepers (SOES), Private security personnel (PASS), Saw-mill workers (TMER), Automobile workers (AUWO), Pappad makers (APLM), Washer men materials (LAWA), Carpenters, Pottery workers (POWO), Press Printing workers (PAPR), Food workers, warehouse workers (LULF), Salt field workers (SALT), Fishermen (FISH), Boat makers (BOAT), Coir makers (COIR), Tannery workers (TALC), Dye (BLDY), Kiln workers (BRIT), Forest products (FORP), Cashew industries (CASH), Distribution of cooking gas cylinders (LPGC), Cycle rickshaw workers (MAFW), Crackers and Safety matches workers (MAFW), Cloth presser (FOTG), Gunny bags manufacturers (GUNI), Goldsmiths (GSAM), Ironsmiths (NEET), Palm water products (NIBG), Workers of flour & Rice Mills (FURD), powerloom workers (PRIL), Waste materials pickers (RAPI), Stage makers (SAGO), Synthetic jem cutters (SYSGM), Sericulture workers (SREE), Tin makers (TINC), Varian makers (VEMA), Sculptures (SCLP), Workers in

Handicraft Industry (HAND), Workers in liquor industries (CIGR), Artists (ARTS), Videographics & Photo graphers (VIPH), Electricians services (ELSR), Folklore artisans (FULR) and the like. Among all the above mentioned works except a very few works, majority of them are also done by the female workers.

The unorganized labour accounted for more than 96 per cent of the total workforce according to census 2001. The majority of women workers come under this category and is employed in the rural areas. Among the rural women workers, 87 per cent are employed in agriculture as labourers and cultivators. In the urban areas, 80 per cent of the women workers are employed in household industries, petty traders, domestic servants and workers in the cottage industries. Though women constitute a significant part of workforce, they lag behind men and they are the neglected section of the society. Moreover, it is an established fact that women bear a disproportionately heavy burden of work than men as they have to contribute more time in the care economy that is the domestic work.

Nature of Women's Employment

The process of Liberalization, Globalization and Privatization has necessitated women's participation in the labour market. Traditionally their occupational status has always been associated with the home and family. But over the years, the pressure of population and economic compulsions, educational and social changes have necessitated a change in women's status and their role, which was hitherto that of a house wife. Women participation in remunerated work in the formal and non-formal labour market has increased significantly. They have become increasingly involved in micro, small and medium, sized enterprises. Women's share in the labourforce continues to rise and almost everywhere more women are working outside the household. There is no job, which they cannot aspire. There is no political office they cannot achieve. There is an increasing number of women engaged in white coller jobs.

Economic liberalization or reforms lead to the growth in service industries such as data processing, tourism, telecommunications and finance where women are preferred as secretaries, receptionists, hostesses and stenographers. Women workers are preferred in such type of employments and jobs as they are considered as a major source of flexible labour. At present the young women from upper and middle class families are joining the workforce in increasing numbers adding a new dimension to their age-old roles as wife and mother. Those who work in unorganized sector also suffer from many problems. In this context it is felt to have a study about unorganized workers.

Problems and Women Workers

It is a recognized fact that there is still no society in the world in which women workers enjoy the same opportunities as men. The women unorganized sector are facing many problems. According to the 2001 census about 96 per cent of women workers in India are in the unorganized sector. The rise of female participating in unorganized sector is due to the compulsion and employer's preference for female employee. Their ignorance, illiteracy and poverty have added fuel to their woes all the more. Women are considered the human resource of choice for the unorganized sector because they lack education and training and are amenable to accept lower wages for equal work due to gender casting. On the basis of Government reports the major problems faced by women are:

1. Women have to work under very poor working and living conditions.
2. Women workers are paid lower and marginal wages.
3. They have to work for long hours even forced to work in late night without protection.
4. They suffer from job insecurity and under-employment.
5. They are deprived of adequate social security, safety and welfare provisions.
6. They are not protected by any government labour organizations.
7. They have to face sexual harassment at the workplace.
8. They have lack of outside linkages and opportunities.
9. There is no job security.

A study was conducted in Theni District regarding the problems faced by the womenfolk. A sample of 200 women workers working in various industries located in and around Theni, were selected at random by applying convenient sampling technique. The various problems faced by these workers were identified by having conversations with them many a times. The problems were studied through an opinion survey prepared for this purpose, in the study area. The respondents were asked to rank each problem identified for this purpose in the order of importance.

The various problems of the respondents of the study were tested with the help of Garrett's ranking technique. This method was suggested by Garrett for ascertaining the ranks into scores when number of items ranked differed from respondents to respondents. The per cent position for each rank was found using the following formula:

$$\text{Per cent position} = \frac{100(Rij - 0.5)}{Nj}$$

Where

Rij = Rank given to ith factor by *j*th individual

Nj = Number of factors ranked by *j*th individual

By referring to the table by Garrett, the per cent positions estimated were converted into scores. Then for each factor, scores of various respondents were added and divided by the number of respondents to arrive at the mean score. The mean score thus obtained for each factor were arranged in descending order. The factor with highest mean score was given the first rank, followed by second, third and so on. It is to be noted that under each problem the respondents were asked to give only one rank to a factor.

The various problems faced by the workers were categorized as problems relating to:

1. Working Conditions
2. Living Conditions
3. Time of Work
4. Remuneration

5. Security
6. Harassment
7. Protection of Rights

1. Working Conditions

The various causes pertaining to Working Conditions include less hygiene prevails, old machines, time taken is more, low wages, insecurity, old technology and no latest technology. In order to highlight the most dominant cause affecting working conditions in the study area, data were interpreted by using Garrett's Ranking Technique and the results are presented in Table 6.1.

Table 6.1: Working Condition Related Causes

Cause	*Garrett's Mean Score*	*Rank*
Less hygiene prevails	64.80	I
Old machines	61.61	II
Time taken is more	52.77	III
Low wages	44.80	IV
Insecurity	42.10	V
No latest technology	40.81	VI

Source: Computed data.

Table 6.1 reveals that among the causes that are responsible for working conditions, less hygienity ranks first with the highest mean score of 64.80. Old machines is found to be the second ranking cause with 61.61 mean score, followed by time taken is more ranking the third with a mean score of 52.77, low wages ranking fourth with a mean score of 44.80, insecurity ranking fifth with a mean score of 42.10 and no latest technology is ranking sixth with a mean score of 40.81.

2. Living Conditions

The various causes pertaining to Living Conditions include living environment is poor, low income, more dependants, female dominated family and indebtedness. In order to highlight the most dominant cause affecting living conditions in the study area, data were interpreted by using Garrett's Ranking Technique and the results are presented in Table 6.2.

Table 6.2 reveals that among the causes that are responsible for Living Conditions, living environment is poor ranks first with the highest mean score of 60.55. Low income is found to be the second rank with 59.83 mean score, followed by more dependents is ranking the third with a mean score of 52.77, female dominated family ranking fourth with a mean score of 47.62 and indebtedness ranked fifth with a mean score of 42.10.

Table 6.2: Living Condition Related Causes

Cause	*Garrett's Mean Score*	*Rank*
Living environment is poor	60.55	I
Low income	59.83	II
More dependents	52.77	III
Female dominated family	47.62	IV
Indebtedness	42.10	V

Source: Computed data.

3. Time of Work

The various causes pertaining to Time of work include, more hours of work, no over time and shift in work. In order to high light the most dominant cause affecting Time of work in the study area, data were interpreted by using Garrett's Ranking Technique and the results are presented in Table 6.3.

Table 6.3: Time of Work Related Causes

Cause	*Garrett's Mean Score*	*Rank*
More hours of work	61.57	I
No over time	54.62	II
Shift in work	51.04	III

Source: Computed data.

Table 6.3 reveals that among the causes responsible for respondents Time of Work, more hours of work ranks first with the highest mean score of 61.57. No over time to be the second ranking cause with 54.62 mean score, followed by shift in work is ranking the third with a mean score of 51.04

4. Remuneration

The various causes pertaining to Remuneration include moderate remuneration, low bonus, and income disparity, break in getting wages, non-application of laws. In order to highlight the most dominant cause affecting Remuneration in the study area, data were interpreted by using Garrett's Ranking Technique and the results are presented in Table 6.4.

Table 6.4: Remuneration Related Causes

Cause	*Garrett's Mean Score*	*Rank*
Moderate remuneration	63.79	I
Low bonus	59.33	II
Income disparity	51.42	III
Break in getting wages	46.11	IV
Non-application of laws	40.01	V

Source: Computed data.

Table 6.4 reveals that among the causes that are responsible for Remuneration, moderate remuneration ranks first with the highest mean score of 63.79. Low Bonus is found to be the second ranking cause with 59.33 mean score, followed by Income Disparity ranking the third with a mean score of 51.42, break in getting wages ranking fourth with a mean score of 46.11 and non-application of laws is ranking fifth with a mean score of 40.01.

5. Insecurity

The various causes pertaining to Insecurity include legislative insecurity, job insecurity, family insecurity and financial insecurity. In order to highlight the most dominant cause affecting insecurity in the study area, data were interpreted by using Garrett's Ranking Technique and the results are presented in Table 6.5.

Table 6.5 reveals that among the causes that are responsible for Insecurity, Legislative insecurity ranks first with the highest mean score of 56.72. Job insecurity is found to be the second ranking cause with 54.11 mean score, followed by Family insecurity ranking the third with a mean score of 49.37 and the financial insecurity is ranking fourth with a mean score of 41.52.

Table 6.5: Insecurity Related Causes

Cause	*Garrett's Mean Score*	*Rank*
Legislative insecurity	56.72	I
Job insecurity	54.11	II
Family insecurity	49.37	III
Financial insecurity	41.52	IV

Source: Computed data.

6. Harassment

The various causes pertaining to Harassment include sexual harassment, financial harassment, family harassment, caste harassment. In order to highlight the most dominant cause affecting Harassment in the study area, data were interpreted by using Garrett's Ranking Technique and the results are presented in Table 6.6.

Table 6.6: Harassment Related Causes

Cause	*Garrett's Mean Score*	*Rank*
Sexual harassment	57.62	I
Financial harassment	54.59	II
Family harassment	47.60	III
Caste harassment	42.40	IV

Source: Computed data.

Table 6.6 reveals that among the causes that are responsible for Harassment, sexual harassment ranks first with the highest mean score of 57.62. Financial harassment is found to be the second ranking cause with 54.59 mean score, followed by Family harassment ranking the third with a mean score of 47.60 and Caste harassment is ranking fourth with a mean score of 42.40.

7. Protection of Rights

The various causes pertaining to Protection of Rights include salary protection, leave protection, job protection, health protection. In order to highlight the most dominant cause affecting Protection of Rights in the study area, data were interpreted by using Garrett's Ranking Technique and the results are presented in Table 6.7.

Table 6.7: Protection of Rights Related Causes

Cause	*Garrett's Mean Score*	*Rank*
Salary protection	59.72	I
Leave protection	52.61	II
Job protection	48.98	III
Health protection	40.17	IV

Source: Computed data.

Table 6.7 reveals that among the causes that are responsible for Protection of Rights, salary protection ranks first with the highest mean score of 59.72. Leave protection is found to be the second ranking cause with 52.61 mean score, followed by job protection ranking the third with a mean score of 48.98 and health protection is ranking fourth with a mean score of 42.40.

Legislative Security

There are much legislation enacted for the protection and welfare of the workers of the unorganized sector. All the central labour laws are applicable to women workers in unorganized sector. The historic universal Declaration of Human Rights, hailed as the international Magna Carta Mankind is a Bill of Rights which opposes discrimination between the sexes. The Indian Constitution has given due recognition to unorganized women's work. But all these things proved to be failure due to the complex situation of the unorganized sector, the enforcement machinery proves to be ineffective.

The Maternity Benefit Act of 1961 protects the dignity of motherhood by providing the benefit of leave with full wages. The Equal Remuneration Act of 1976 provides the payment of equal remuneration to men and women workers for their same work. In 1997 the Supreme Court of India announced that sexual harassment of working women amounts to be the violation of rights of gender equality. Detailed norms and regulations for the prevention of sexual harassment of women workers at workplace are given under article 141 of the Constitution of India. By noticing the problems of the unorganized sector the Second Labour Commission, 2002 recommended the Umbrella Legislation. It is for the protection and welfare of the workers.

The object of the Umbrella Legislation includes recognition for all workers in unorganized sector, economic and social security, removal of poverty and elimination of child labour. The Unorganized Sector Workers Social Security Scheme (2004) was introduced by the Ministry of Labour of the Government of India. The scheme envisages providing triple benefits in the form of old-age pension, personal accident insurance and universal health insurance.

The Government of India has started many developmental programmes for the economic development of both rural and urban areas. Through the volunteer organizations the Central Social Welfare Board has been trying hard for the development of the poor and needy women by helping them in setting up various income generating units. The poverty eradication programmes like Gramodaya Yojana (2000), Samporan Grameen Rojgar Yojana (2001) are providing employment opportunities and social security and also aims to develop empowered women. To meet the credit needs of the poor women the Government set up a Rashtriya Mahila Kosh, a national fund in 1993.

The Indian judiciary has the constitutional mandate to be the custodian of the Fundamental Rights of the individual. It has evolved a unique legal process known as "Public Interest Litigation" apart from the constitutional and legal provisions. Under this process any individual or group can bring to attention of the judiciary cases of violation of human rights of women. The High Court and Supreme Courts take cognizance of such cases and provide remedial measures.

When the individual rights and freedom are seen to be violated, the independent vigilant and vigorous press has acted as a watch dog for the protection of individual rights and freedom. If the human rights are violated by the governmental officers or others, the women workers have to report it to the press or the judiciary for the protection of their rights.

Even after initiating so many developmental programmes and legislative provisions for the women workers in the unorganized sector, a large number of women workers are still highly vulnerable to exploitation. Because they are employed in agriculture, construction and home-based work, which are hard to organize. The Indian Labour Organization reported that the women are disproportionately involved in more precarious and vulnerable forms of employment. They are driven to the apparent refuge provided by self-employment in the poor rural and urban areas. Because of the less income earned by the husband, women are forced to work in order to fulfill the demands of the family. But they were exploited in the working areas. They have no recourse for any remedies owing to the invisible and unorganized nature of their work.

Steps to be Taken

The empowerment of women is an important necessity of the present day. The efforts of the government to improve the conditions of the women workers are praiseworthy. But due to the corrupt practices of the functionaries the beneficiaries are not capable to utilize these programmes. The efforts of the government proved tot be failure. In order to improve the conditions of unorganized women workers some of the suggestions are recommended:

- Women workers should be educated and make them aware about their rights and legislative provisions.
- Effective steps should be taken to reflect the duty of the government and society to protect the Human Rights of Women workers.
- The legislations, which prevent all forms of discriminations and guarantee equal job opportunities, should be strictly enacted and implemented.

- To protect the human rights of unorganized women workers, necessary amendments are required to be made in the labour laws.
- For the payment of compensation in case of injury or exploitation in unorganized sector, a Compensation Board be formed.
- Women must be motivated to utilize the existing programmes.
- To fight against the discriminations and exploitation, the women workers must be encouraged to form groups.
- Conduct Human rights educating camps at regular intervals and strengthen the Human Rights Commission to protect the vulnerable section of women workers.
- There should be a proper regulation of unorganized sector industries, which will assume women workers job security, healthy work environment and at least minimum wages, maternity and child care benefits.
- Women worker leaders must be included in the policy formulation and other decision-making processes relating to the welfare of the women workers.
- The political will of the government, financial resource and self-confidence of the women workers only lead to the improvement of condition not only women but men also have to change their attitudes towards women for their betterment.

Conclusion

The unorganised sector has been most vulnerable and ignored sector in India. It holds an important place in Indian Economy. So the unorganized women workers development should the viewed as an issue in social development to be seen as an essential component in every dimension of development. In order to get empowerment the government and the social workers may contribute significant role in making women workers capable, self reliant and well organized. It is worthwhile to create the awakening among unorganized women so that they can come up by taking care of themselves. Thus, there is no exaggeration in saying that the backbone of Indian workforce is the unorganized sector. Yet there is a tendency to ignore this mass of workforce as these millions who belong to unorganized sector are politically powerless and economically weak. So, there is an urgent need to give top priority to the issues and problems of the workers of unorganized sector.

REFERENCES

1. Government of India 2002, *Report of the Second National Commission on Labour*.
2. *The Economic Times,* dated 26.3.2003.
3. Singh, Sehgal B.P., "*Human Rights in India, Problems and Perspectives.*
4. Narashimha Rao, P.V., "*Human Rights A Reaffirmation.*
5. Jhabvala, R and R.K.A. Suramaniam *The unorganized sector work Security and Social Protection*.
6. D.P. Singh, *Women Workers in Unorganized Sector*.
7. Banerjee, Nirmala: *Women Workers in the Unorganized Sector,* Hyderabad.
8. Desai N: *Women in Modern India,* Bombay
9. Gandhi, M.K.: *Role of Women,* Bombay.
10. Gangrade, K.D: *Women and Child Workers in Unorganized Sector,* New Delhi.
11. *India 2003*—A Reference Annual Government of India, New Delhi.

7

A Study of Cargo Handling Workers in Thoothukudi Port Trust

A Study

Dr. S. Kannan*
Dr. A. Padrakali**

Introduction

The Port of Tuticorin when it was commissioned, did not employ any labourers. They contracted with the TSA (Tuticorin Stewards Association) for this purpose. During 1970s, the Government of India made an Ordinance that all the Major Ports should possess a labour pool to supply labourers for cargo handling. At that time, Tuticorin Port was a weaker port and was in financial deficit. So Tuticorin Port cannot form a labour pool. Instead they relied upon the TSA.

TSA is an association of ship-owners, merchants and businessmen of Tuticorin. They hired thousands of labourers for cargo handling in Port. However, the labourers were not given any assurance of work or wage. The labourers were paid weekly.

---

* **M.Com., Ph.D., D.G.T., Reader in Commerce, Kamaraj College, Thoothukudi *E-mail:* kannansoundrapandian@yahoo.co.in**

** **M.Com, M.Phil., Ph.D., S.G, Lecturer in Commerce, A.P.C. Mahalaxmi College for Women, Thoothukudi – 628 001.**

However, the contract with the TSA was not desired by the labourers and the Port authorities also. The reasons are:

- Labourers under the management of TSA did not get reasonable wages.
- No regular employment. The worker may or may not be given job.
- The TSA administration differentiates the labourers and the labourers, who are well known to them, are called upon for job. So other labourers had no job to do. Due to 'No Work, No Pay' policy, the other labourers suffered a lot.
- Labourers were not given any welfare measures, or social security programmes.
- The Port Management also found difficult to maintain good relations with the TSA.
- TSA did not supply labourers at the right time. This made the Port a very heavy damage.
- Contractual labourers did not work upto the standards and needs of the Port.

Therefore all the labourers under the TSA demanded the Port Authorities to merge the labourers with the Tuticorin Port Trust.

The then Tuticorin Port Trust Chairman Mr. Machendra Nathan, IAS, had made an agreement with the TSA and formed the TPTCHLP (Tuticorin Port Trust Cargo Handling Labour Pool). All the labourers working under the TSA were merged with the TPTCHLP.

Cargo Handling Labour Pool

Tuticorin Port Trust Cargo Handling Labour Pool was commissioned on 27th October, 1981 with 3600 labourers. However, only from January 2000, Tuticorin Port Trust took over the control and management of TPTCHLP. TPTCHLP does not receive any benefit or grant from Tuticorin Port Trust or the Government of India. It operates under a 'Self Financed Scheme'.

When a ship or cargo vessel arrives at the Port, it pays certain amount for the usage of Port, levy, labour handling charge etc. Traffic Department of the TPT collects them and puts in a pool. From this fund, the TPTCHLP gets its share for supplying labourers. TPTCHLP pay the amount as wages for the labourers.

The present study is an attempt to examine the socio-economic conditions of the cargo handling labourers in Tuticorin Port Trust.

Statement of the Problem

Port Trust has been functioning as a Central Government organization also enjoying monopoly rights. The central governments earns a huge profit from custom's duty of exports and imports. In cargo handling there are greater chances for accidents and deaths. In this type work unless proper labour measures are given the workers may not like to work. A proper study shall bring out the problems of cargo handling workers and their attitude towards employment. The present study is an attempt in this direction.

Scope of the Study

The study is an attempt to understand the workers attitude towards their employment conditions in Tuticorin Port Trust.

Objectives

1. To study the socio-economic conditions of the cargo handling labourers in Tuticorin Port Trust.
2. To study the problems of labourers.
3. To offer suggestions to improve the status of labourers.

Methodology

The study was based on the survey method. The primary data has been collected from the cargo handling labourers of Port Trust with the help of an interview schedule. Secondary data has been collected from the articles, journals and the books.

Sampling Design

At present there are, 1263 employees of which 1206 were cargo handling labourers involved Tuticorin Port. Among them

120 cargo handling labourers were taken as the sample size. For selecting the sample labourers Convenient Sampling Technique has been adopted.

Study Period

The study was made during the months of November to March 2006.

Social Background of the Workers

The social background of the workers shall be studied under the heads namely, name, age, literacy level, experience, size of the family. They are presented in the succeeding pages.

Age of Labourers

Labourers of different age groups involved in Port Trust. The Table 7.1 lists out the age groups of labourers involved in Port Trust.

Table 7.1: Age of Labourers

Age	*No. of labourers*	*Per cent*
Below 30	6	5
30-40	20	17
40-50	54	45
Above 50	40	33
Total	**120**	**100**

Source: Primary data.

Table 7.1 discloses the fact that the labourers in the age group of 40-50 years constitute 45 per cent. Labourers in the age group of above 50 years constitute 33 per cent. Labourers in the age group of 30-40 years constitute 17 per cent. Remaining 5 per cent of labourers are in the age group, below 30 years. It could be inferred that the largest proportion of the labourers are in the age group of 40-50 years.

Literacy Level of Labourers

To have a detailed study of the labourers, their literacy level should be studied. Table 7.2 shows the literacy level of TPT labourers.

Table 7.2: Literacy Level of Labourers

Level	*No. of labourers*	*Per cent*
Illiterate	27	23
Up to High School	61	51
Up to Higher Secondary	28	23
Above Higher Secondary	–	–
Technical Qualification	4	3
Total	**120**	**100**

Source: Primary data.

The able 7.2 reveals the fact that 51 per cent of TPT labourers has been educated upto high school level. 23 per cent of labourers form the level of higher secondary education. 23 per cent of labourers are illiterate people. 3 per cent of labourers have technical qualification. It could be understood that greater proportion of workers literacy level is upto high school level only. The lower literacy level may be the reason for poor economic status of TPT labourers.

Size of the Family of Labourers

Table 7.3 discloses the size of the family of TPT labourers. The size of the family of TPT labourers are as follows.

Table 7.3: Size of the Family of Labourers

Size	*No. of labourers*	*Per cent*
Below 3	8	7
4	28	23
5	38	32
6	29	24
Above 6	17	14
Total	**120**	**100**

Source: Primary data.

Table 7.3 shows that 32 per cent of the labourers have 5 members in their family. 24 per cent of the labourers have 6 members in their family. 23 Per cent of the labourers have 4 family members. 14 per cent of labourers have more than 6 family members. The remaining 7 per cent of the labourers have less than 3 members. It is clear that larger proportion of the workers have larger family (with more than 5 members).

Year of Experience

The Table 7.4 describes the years of experience of TPT labourers.

Table 7.4: Year of Experience

Years of experience	*No. of labourers*	*Per cent*
Below 5 years	30	25
5-10 years	14	12
10-15 years	19	16
15-20 years	21	17
20-25 years	24	20
Above 25 years	12	10
Total	**120**	**100**

The Table 7.4 discloses the fact that 25 per cent of labourers have less than 5 years of experience. 20 per cent of labourers have 20-25 years of experience. 17 per cent of the labourers have 15-20 years of experience. 16 per cent of labourers have 10-15 years of experience. 12 per cent of labourers have 5-10 years of experience. Remaining 10 per cent of them have more than 25 years of experience. This shows that in recent years greater proportion of labourers entered into the cargo handling pool.

Category of Labourers

The labourers' involvement depends upon the type of work. The details about the nature of job the labourers undertake are enquired. Table 7.5 describes the different types of labourers.

Table 7.5: Category of Labourers

Category	*No. of labourers*	*Per cent*
Mazdoor	36	30
Maistry	8	7
Tally clerk	12	10
Signal man	23	19
Winch man	35	29
Board supervisor	6	5
Total	**120**	**100**

Source: Primary data.

Table 7.5 reveals that 30 per cent of the labourers are belonging to mazdoor. 29 per cent of the labourers are doing the work of winch man. 19 per cent of the labourers are doing the work of signal man. Next 10 per cent of the labourers are involved in the job of tally clerk. Another 7 per cent of the labourers are involved in the work of Maistry. Remaining 5 per cent of labourers are under the category of Board supervisor. It could be inferred that the largest proportion of labourers are under the category of mazdoor.

Salary of Labourers

This Table 7.6 shows the monthly salary earned by the TPT labourers.

Table 7.6: Monthly Salary of Labourers

Salary Rs.	*No of labourers*	*Per cent*
11000-12000	62	52
12000-13000	48	40
13000-14000	10	8
Total	**120**	**100**

Source: Primary data.

The above Table 7.6 discloses the fact about the salary of the TPT labourers. 52 per cent of labourers are earning a monthly salary of Rs. 11000-12000. Next 40 per cent of labourers are earning a monthly salary of Rs. 12000-13000. Remaining 8 per cent of labourers are earning a monthly salary of Rs. 13000-14000. There is no labourers earning a monthly salary of 14000-15000 and more than 15000.

Residence of Labourers

Table 7.7 reveals the residence of labourers of TPT. It discloses whether the TPT labourers are living in the rented houses or in their own houses or the quarters given by TPT.

Table 7.7: Residence of Labourers

Residence	*No. of labourers*	*Per cent*
Rented House	31	26
Own House	89	74
Quarters	–	–
Total	**120**	**100**

Source: Primary data.

The Table 7.7 describes the residence of the labourers of TPT. 74 per cent of them are living in their own houses. 26 per cent of them are living in the rental houses. None of them are living in quarters because the TPT did not provide quarters for the labourers.

Source of Welfare Measures

Table 7.8 throws light on the fact how labour welfare measures in TPT are satisfied through authorities.

Table 7.8: Source of Welfare Measures

Initiatives for welfare measures	*No. of labourers*	*Per cent*
Trade Union	65	54
Management	52	43
Labour Welfare Legislation	3	3
Central and State Govt. Policies	–	–
Total	**120**	**100**

Source: Primary data.

Table 7.8 reveals the fact how the labourers are getting their needs or welfare measures. 54 per cent of the labourers revealed the fact they are getting their needs or welfare measures through Trade Union. 43 per cent of the labourers opined that they get their welfare measures done through the management of TPT. Remaining 3 per cent of labourers feel that they get these welfare measures because of labour welfare legislation. Thus it could be understood that the workers do not get wages because of central and state government policies.

Satisfaction of Labour Welfare Measures

This Table 7.9 shows the satisfaction of labour welfare measures on the 3 scale methods.

Table 7.9: Satisfaction of Labour Welfare Measures

Labour Welfare Measure	*Highly satisfied*	*%*	*Satisfied*	*%*	*Not Satisfied*	*%*	*Total*	*%*
Loan Facilities	54	45	61	51	5	4	120	100
Free Medical Assistance	66	55	46	38	8	7	120	100
Educational Assistance	17	14	69	58	34	28	120	100
Leave Travel Concession	29	24	71	59	20	17	120	100
Washing Facilities	18	15	71	59	31	26	120	100
Facilities for Sitting	57	48	51	42	12	10	120	100
Canteen Facilities	60	50	52	43	8	7	120	100
Restroom facilities	50	42	64	53	6	5	120	100
First Aid facilities	58	48	60	50	2	2	120	100
Community Hall	21	17	63	53	36	30	120	100
Packaged Drinking Water	41	34	37	31	42	35	120	100
Job Training	26	22	73	61	21	17	120	100
Safety Equipments	67	56	41	34	12	10	120	100
Uniforms	54	45	58	48	8	7	120	100
Counseling	26	22	52	43	42	35	120	100
Accident Insurance	54	45	55	46	11	9	120	100
Wages for the Sickness Period	28	23	60	50	32	27	120	100

Source: Computed Data.

Table 7.9 reveals the fact that some labour welfare measures provided to the labourers are highly satisfied. 55 per cent of labourers are satisfied with free medical assistance, 48 per cent of labourers are satisfied with the waiting room , 50 per cent of labourers are satisfied with canteen facilities, similarly 56 per cent of labourers are satisfied with safety equipments.

Labourers are satisfied with some of the labour measures. They are of loan facilities (51%), Educational assistance (58%), 59 per cent, Insurance facilities, washing facilities (59%), community hall (53%), Job training (61%), Uniforms (48%), counseling (43%) wages for the sickness period (50%). Remaining welfare measures are not satisfactory to the labourers. That is drinking water facility is not adequate.

Working Environment

This Table 7.10 and Fig. 7.1 reveals the workers attitude towards the Work Environment in Tuticorin Port Trust.

Table 7.10: Working Environment

Environment	*Good*	%	*Fair*	%	*Bad*	%	*Total*	%
Clean Environment	50	42	58	48	12	10	120	100
Safety Environment	48	40	61	51	11	9	120	100
Accident Free Zone	17	14	47	39	56	47	120	100
Not safer	19	16	43	36	58	48	120	100
Not Hygienic	3	3	17	14	100	83	120	100

Source: Primary data.

Table 7.10 describes the working environment. 42 per cent of workers feel that the environment is clean. From the safety point of view, 40 per cent of labourers opined that the environment is good, 51 per cent are of opinion that environment is fair and 9 per cent of the labourers feel that the work environment is bad. This shows that their working in TPT is accident prone. But the environment is very clean and neat.

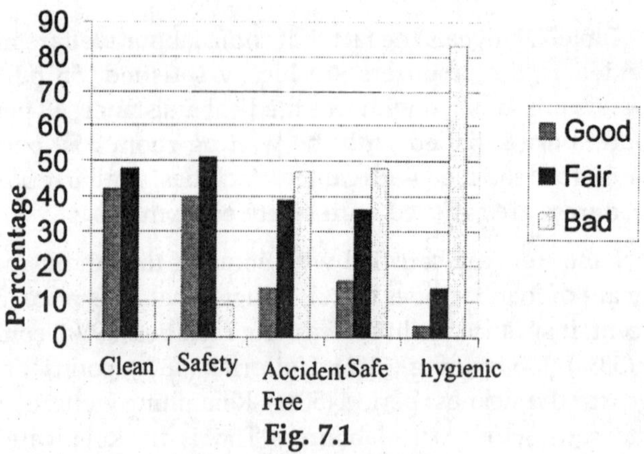

Fig. 7.1
Working Environment

Chances of Accident

The Table 7.11 and Fig. 7.2 reveals the fact about the Chances of Accidents.

Table 7.11: Chances of Accident

Chances of Accident	*No. of labourers*	*%*
Very High	19	16
High	41	34
Moderate	24	20
Low	22	18
Very Low	14	12
Total	**120**	**100**

Source: Primary data.

Table 7.11 shows that 34 per cent of labourers feels that there have greater chances for accident. 20 per cent of labourers feel that the chances of accident are normal. Another 18 per cent of them are of opinion that the chances are low.

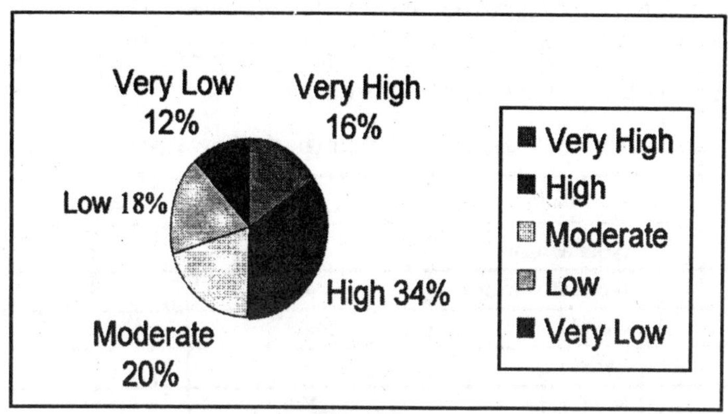

Fig. 7.2
Chances of Accident

Expectation of New Welfare Scheme

This Table 7.12 shows the expectations of labourers about New Welfare Scheme.

Table 7.12: Expectation of New Welfare Scheme

New Welfare Schemes	*No. of labourers*	*Per cent*
Job assurance and security	31	26
Family members medical check up	11	9
Children's education facility	4	3
Quarters	13	11
High salary	29	24
Canteen	–	–
All the above	32	27
Total	**120**	**100**

Source: Primary data.

Table 7.12 describes that 27 per cent of labourers expect all the new welfare schemes to them. 26 per cent of them are expecting job assurances and security. 24 per cent are expecting high salary. 11 per cent of them expect quarters for living. 9 per cent of the workers expect the medical check up for all the family members. Remaining 3 per cent of them are expecting children's education facilities.

Management's Approach towards Labourers

Table 7.13 reveals the labourers opinion regarding the approach of management towards labourers.

Table 7.13: Management's Approach Towards Labourers

Opinion	*No. of labourers*	*Per cent*
Satisfactory	51	43
Not satisfactory	6	5
Good	36	30
Bad	1	1
Moderate	26	21
Total	**120**	**100**

Table 7.13 reveals the fact that 43 per cent of labourers are satisfied about the approach of management. 30 per cent of labourers feel that the approach of management is good. Another 21 per cent of workers opine that the approach to workers is moderate. Only 5 per cent of workers are not satisfied with the attitude of management, remaining 1 per cent feel that the management relationship with workers is bad. From this it could be understood that the management's approach towards labourers is very much satisfactory as larger proportion of workers opine that the management maintain cordial relationship with workers.

Findings of the Study

The present study has unveiled the following facts.

- Majority of the labourers are in the age group of 40-50 years.
- Majority of the labourers have high school education. It is understood that they have much knowledge about their work.
- Among 120 sample respondents 32 per cent of the labourers have 5 members in their family.
- Most of the labourers are living in their own houses (74%).
- The largest proportion of the labourers have only 5 years of experience in their work (25%).
- Among the different category of labourers 30 per cent of the labourers are Mazdoor.

- Majority of the labourers are earning a monthly salary of 11000-12000.
- Most of the labourers are highly satisfied about their welfare measures.
- Majority of the labourers say that the working environment is bad.
- There are more chances for accidents in cargo handlings (34%).
- More number of labourers said that at present the welfare measures are good.

Suggestions

- To concentrate fully on the work, the environment must be improved more. So that the labourers' work will be more efficient.
- While handling cargos more accidents are happening. To lessen the accidents preventive measures must be taken. The study suggests to adopt new technologies to reduce the number of accidents.
- The labourers are in need of more welfare measures in their occupation . So this study suggests that more welfare measures shall be developed and to be implemented.
- The labourers shall be provided with quarters.

Conclusion

Cargo handling is an accident prone job. Despite the invent of modern technologies, the presence of labourers in handling cargo is inevitable. Cargo handling is a laborious job. Even though they work hard, the economic conditions of the workers are not upto satisfactory level. Therefore their needs must be fulfilled by offering more labour welfare measures. If workers are satisfied, the productivity of TPT improve more than today's condition.

REFERENCE

Annual Reports of the Tuticorin Port Trust Various Issues, 2000-2004.

8

A Study on Hawkers in Tiruchendur

Dr. S. Narayana Rajan*

Abstract

Hawking is the major business of the middle and lower income group of people in major Indian cities. Mumbai has the largest number of hawkers numbering around two lakhs . Both in urban and rural areas, most of the hawkers have the direct link with retailers. They are the independent, informal units of retail business in India . The recent developments in the retail business brings high pressure to the hawking community. In retail business, the nature of demand is changing with the entry of large corporates into organised retailing to meet the higher aspirants of the consumers with more buying power. Nowadays, retail business is actually attracting the major international players. This brings a tremendous change in the development of retail business. Since, India is a country with diverse demographic differences, the impact of shopping malls on hawking business should also be studied for taking right measures to develop hawking business, as it is the life blood of the poor and middle income groups. This

* **M.B.A, Ph.D, Reader, Department of Business Administration, Aditanar College of Arts and Science, Virapandian Patnam, Tiruchendur, Thoothukudi District, Tamilnadu – 628 216**
E-mail: **nelkavi@yahoo.com**

paper seeks to bring out the picture about the present status of Indian hawkers in rural areas and also the importance of hawking in the development of Indian business.

Hawkers – An Overview

The traders who walk around the village, town or city offering goods and services without a fixed place is known as "Hawkers". These movable vendors earn their income depending upon their skills and also the capacities to identify the appropriate consumer.

The hawkers can be classified into movable hawkers and also stationary hawkers. Even though mobility is the significant character of hawkers, some hawkers develop friendship and human relations in particular area. This improves their popularity and compel some to stay in the same location. They also identify the suitable location for their business and generate goodwill among the customers. These hawkers are called stationary hawkers.

Hawkers are playing an important role in rural and urban economy of India. More than 50 per cent of the labourforce are in urban areas of major cities like Chennai, Mumbai, Kolkata and Delhi. This urban labourforce forms an informal urban sector which works for its livelihood. Among the people of this sectors, illiterates and educated youths become hawkers. The unemployment problems persisting in cities and also unemployability of youth, force the people to prefer hawking. But in cities hawking is considered as an illegal activity in most of the important places. However, local authorities of villages and towns recognize hawking as a legal activity.

Objectives

The following are the major objectives of this study:

1. To study about the level of hawking business in India.
2. To identify the type of hawkers in Tiruchendur.
3. To analyse the problems of hawkers.
4. To find out the ways and means to improve the business of hawking in Tiruchendur.

Methodology

This study is compiled with the help of both primary and secondary data. The primary data were collected directly from respondents with the help of structured interview. Secondary data were collected from books and journals.

The variable to be studied were identified in the preliminary interview conducted with some selected respondents who involve themselves in hawking.

The variables so identified in the preliminary interview were covered by appropriate questions. A pre-test was conduted. In the light of the experience gained through the pre-test, necessary modifications were made.

This study comprises of people of Tiruchendur in Thoothukudi district of Tamilnadu who engage themselves in hawking. Since the population varies, based on seasons and also festivals in Lord Subramania Swamy Temple of Tiruchendur, Convinience sampling technique has been adopted to select the sample respondents. However, care has been taken to include the sample respondents from all types of hawking business such as florist, photographers, palm analyst etc.

The sampling unit is the individual respondent. The size of the sample is 125, decided arbitrarily. The researcher carried out his field work for this study during the period from June 2008 to August 2008.

Hawkers in India

Hawking is regarded as an illegal activity in some of the major cities, like Mumbai, Kolkatta, Bangalore and Chennai. The local authorities and police impose more restrictions on their business. There is no ban for hawking, but their activities are restricted. They are not allowed to use the urban space like parks, gardens, markets, educational institutions, hospitals, administrative offices, railway stations to do their business. Even in rural areas the authorities informally impose certain restrictions in their trade. Hawkers, with the pressures from internal and external forces , are coming from within and outside India.

The following are some of the important guidelines for hawking, issued by the Supreme Court of India.

(a) Roads and footpaths are for commuting. Hawking is not a fundamental right. Hawkers can not claim a right to any public place.

(b) Mumbai to be divided into Hawking Zones, Prohibited Zones, and Rest of the City.

(c) Hawking zones to have demarcated pitches on roads selected as per stated criteria. This would accommodate around 23,000 hawkers, selected by lottery every year.

(d) In prohibited zones e.g. around railway stations, hospitals, schools, colleges, religious places, high-security places, no hawking to be permitted.

(e) Elsewhere in the city, roving hawkers to be freely allowed. No limit on numbers. Anyone can get a licence.

The following are the recommendations of Supreme Court:

(a) In areas other than hawking, and no-hawking, hawking to be allowed in 'temporarily' demarcated spots/stretches.

(b) The number of hawkers, timings, types of goods sold, etc. to be as decided by a broad-based Ward Hawker Committee in each ward.

(c) The number of hawkers to be upto 1 per 1000 adult population i.e. upto 50 per Councillor Ward.

(d) Other special ways to hawk to be looked into, e.g. hawkers plazas/markets, weekly bazaars, khau gallis, in private premises, festival licences, etc. as decided by the Ward Hawker Committee.

(e) To avoid unnecessarily receiving an unmanageable number of applications every year, criteria such as eligibility (domicile), conditions (type of goods), and preferences (disabled, women above 50, men above 60), and recommendations from nearby residents (for 'temporary' areas) to be included.

(f) Strictly roving hawkers, i.e. who engage in door-to-door service need not have to get a licence, as they are using the roads/footpaths for transportation just as delivery-boys do, and not for selling. (There too, however, be an enabling clause for licences for the future.) This also accommodates the remainder of the existing hawkers.

(g) A City Hawker Committee to oversee the overall implementation and co-ordination and supervision of the 24 Ward Hawker Committees.

The hawking community in India faces severe treat to do their business due to strict guidelines of court and local authorities.

Hawkers in Tiruchendur

In Tamilnadu, Thoothukudi district has a good percentage of population hailing from all the 3 sections—lower, middle and the upper section of the society. In Thoothukudi district, Tiruchendur is a very good business centre and there exists many government estabilishments, educational institutions, and a few top operating private firms. Lord Subramania Swamy temple, one of the famous pilgrim centres is located here. Moreover, Tiruchendur is considered as one of the important tourist places in Thoothukudi district. There are thousands of hawkers engaging themselves in different business. Hence this study aims at exploring the problems and prospects of hawkers in Tiruchendur.

There are different types of hawkers in Tiruchendur. They are:

1. Florist
2. Photographers
3. Ice Cream Hawkers
4. Parrot astrologist, palm analyst
5. Devotional cassette sellers
6. Bangle sellers
7. Key chain, electronic watch and pen sellers
8. Photo and toys sellers
9. Devotional photos, dollars and book sellers
10. Tea, coffee, sukkuwater hawkers

11. Footwear sellers
12. T-shirt sellers
13. Decorative light sellers
14. Small vessel sellers
15. Sweet sellers
16. Snack sellers
17. Fruits sellers
18. Vegetable sellers
19. Eatable sellers

These hawkers can be classified into **Movable Hawkers** and also **Stationary Hawkers**. Some of the movable hawkers are florist, photographers, ice cream hawkers , devotional cassette sellers, tea, coffee, sukkuwater hawkers, snack sellers.

The stationary hawkers include parrot astrologist, palm analyst, bangle sellers, key chain sellers, electronic watch and pen seller, photo and toys seller, footwear sellers, t-shirt sellers, decorative light sellers, small vessel sellers, fruits sellers vegetable sellers and eatable sellers.

Findings

Based on the survey of hawkers in Tiruchendur, the findings are classified as follows.

Social Composition

The survey shows that 11 per cent of the hawkers belonged to general caste. 68 per cent were in the OBC category and the remaining 21 per cent comprised of scheduled castes. The largest group of hawkers are in the backward class, because the research area population is coming under the economical reconstruction.

Sex Composition

It is found that 88 per cent males are engaged in hawking, and 12 per cent are the females. Female participation in the business is very low due to the pre-occupation of female members of hawking family. It is also observed that the female participation in hawking was high in the past decades. But due to the socio-cultural changes in Tiruchendur, female participation in hawking is decreasing in recent days. However, the female members in their family are also supporting the male members to do their business successfully in spite of the harassments from different quarters such as the police and the authorities.

Literacy Level

Literacy level of the hawkers in Tiruchendur showed that 17 per cent were illeterate while 52 per cent had their primary education and others 31 per cent had studied up to high school level.

Income Level

The average income of the hawkers was Rs. 45 per day i.e. the monthly average income was around Rs. 1350.

Working Capital

Most of the hawkers raised their working capital with the help of moneylenders who charged high rate of interest. 84 per cent of the hawkers are dependent on the moneylenders. Only 9 per cent took loans from friends, relatives and self-help groups. The interest charged for the loan is very low in self-help group than the moneylenders.

Working Conditions

Most of the hawkers in Tiruchendur live within 10 kilometres radius of Tiruchendur. 61 per cent of them travel at least 10 kilometres to reach their home. 17 per cent of the hawkers travel upto 30 kms. everyday. The working hours range from 5 a.m to 10.30 p.m. Majority of the hawkers concentrate in their business in and around near Subramania Swamy Temple. So their business and working hours are based upon the pooja hours and festival days of the temple.

The hawkers of Tiruchendur suffer a lot with economic, social and cultural problems. The environment for hawking is not favourable. It creates a depression in their income and acts as a barrier for their entrepreneurial potential. They have no fixed working hours and some hawkers work for a maximum of 16 hours daily. Headache, fever, urinary problems, skin diseases, jaundice are some of the common diseases for hawkers that create severe health problems. Some local authorities informally collect Rs. 200 to 500 per/month from the hawkers. Many of them, especially snack vendors lose a lot more by way of force often in kind demanded by local authorities. This leads to a heavy loss of income in this business.

Most of the hawkers are in stress due to non-stability of their income. They earn disrespect from the public due to the lower economic condition. Devoting less time for participating in family functions creates social problem in their life. Most of the hawkers involve their heirs in their own business of hawking even from childhood due to poverty.

(a) It is observed that even the school going students involve themselves in hawking on part time basis. They engage themselves in selling flowers , Tea, Coffee, Vada, Puffs and other related eatables in the morning and in the evening hours also, apart from their study timings. Hawking provides money for their family livelihood.

(b) The photographer hawking community in Tiruchendur do their business near Tiruchendur Subramania Swamy Temple, because their business fully depends upon the pilgrims and also on the devotees of the temple.

(c) It is inferred that the hawkers in Tiruchendur enjoy their maximum business in the month of April and May. However, in December and January their business reaches its height due to the Iyyappa devotees.

(d) The irregular demand of their products, creates loss in their business. It drags their income to the lowest place in their graph and most of the hawkers live below the poverty line.

Suggestions

The following are some of the suggestions for improving hawking business in Tiruchendur.

(a) The authorities may issue license to the hawkers by legalising their business. This will reduce the harassment of the authorities.

(b) This informal sector should be treated as a formal sector so that hawking may be regulated with proper rules and regulation. When it is regulated and organised, the problems of the hawkers may be avoided.

(c) In order to avoid the institutional credit facility, proper guidelines should be framed with the help of local authorities.

(d) N.G.Os and self-help groups should conduct awareness and training programmes for upgrading the knowledge of the hawkers.

(e) The impact of foreign malls should be made known to the hawkers and alternative business arrangements may be made to them by the government.

(f) Special insurance scheme should be designed for the hawkers to meet the losses due to uncertain events.

REFERENCES

1. Sharit Bhowmik , "Hawkers in the Urban Informal Sector—A Study of Street Vendors in Six Cities", National Alliance Street Vendors of India. www.nasvi.net

2. Census Survey of Hawkers on Municipal Lands—by TATA Institute of Social Science and Youth for Unity and Voluntary Action.

3. Mumbai Metropolitan Region Development Authority (MMRDA) Mumbai—plan for 2005.

4. *Franchise Plus*, May-June 2007, Volume 4 Issue 2.

9

The Plight of Salt Workers in Salt Industries in Thoothukudi District

Dr. A. Selva Kumar*

Abstract

Salt is a very essential dietary commodity. Salt is not found in nature straight way in a condition fit for immediate use like rain water or fruits. It is abundantly available and it is in fact an unfailing commodity. But still it can't be used as it is found in nature. Therefore man has devised means of extracting salt from what is a compound in nature. Salt is a cheap and bulk commodity. It is produced in our country by the private, co-operative and government sectors. Prior to independence, salt was imported in the country. India now ranks fourth in the world in the production of salt. Thoothkudi occupies a unique position in salt industries in India because of its geographic location and other favourable factors. In Thoothukudi district, a great number of salt industries are at Mullakaddu, Thirespuram, Muthaiahpuram, Veplaodai, Pazhayakayal, Arumuganeri and Kayalpattnam. In these areas about 44000 adult workers both male and female are working.

* **Reader in Commerce, Pope's College, Sawyerpuram, Thoothukudi District, Tamil Nadu - 628 251.**

***E-mail:* iamaskumar@rediffmail.com, Mobile No: 9442063330.**

More than 100 salt industries are involved in producing salt. The salt industry in the study area is about 5000 acres. The unique character of the salt industry in that it is less capital-intensive and more employment-generating. It provides employment to a large number of skilled and unskilled workers. Workers are employed in maramathu, watering, scraping, removing and other types in the transport and distribution processes. This industry plays a vital role in Tamilnadu's economy and it provides employment and a source of living to a very large number of people for whom there is no other alternative livelihood.

Introduction

Salt is a very essential dietary commodity. Salt is not found in nature straight way in a condition fit for immediate use like rain water or fruits. It is abundantly available and it is in fact an unfailing commodity. But still it can't be used as it is found in nature. Therefore man has devised means of extracting salt from what is a compound in nature. Therefore man has denied means of extracting salt from what is compound in nature.

Salt though available in abundant quantities in sea water, acquires value when manufactured and rendered directly edible. It is this process which renders salt liable for taxation. The salt had been first taxed under Muslim rule and the British Government retained it. Mahatma Gandhi first objected the salt tax. He also violated the Salt Acts. He started the salt " *Satyagraha movement* " in 11th year 1930. After a very long struggle the British Government had withdrawn the salt tax and permitted the local people to manufacture salt from Feb. 1931.

Common salt is an article of daily necessity for human consumption. It has been an important commodity for hundred of years. Common salt is essential for man and other animals. It is used as table salt, daily salt, health salt and salt for cattle fodder. It is used widely in the chemical industry and has various industrial uses.

The importance of salt has tremendously increased in recent years. It is considered to be the basic as well as a highly indispensable commodity. In man's life, in our day-to day life, vegetable without salt is tasteless. It is essential for the maintenance of good health. However, salt can be consumed by both rich and poor family to the limited and fixed quantity irrespective of the price.

Likewise, the availability of salt is only restricted to certain places in our country, depending upon the weather conditions and the availability of salt water for productions. In India, salt is mainly produced out of sea water through solar evaporation.

Salt is a cheap and bulk commodity. It is produced in our country by the private, co-operative and government sectors. Prior to independence, salt was imported in the country. India now ranks fourth in the world in the production of salt. Consequently, salt is now being exported after meeting the demand inside the country. The other countries which have higher rates are the U.S.A., Germany and China. Our country is blessed with a long coastal line of about 5600 k.m. Therefore the bulk of salt productions in our country is from marine sources. Salt is not manufactured in all places because it's productions requires special weather and social conditions. Moreover, salt production is also seasonal in character due to frequent rainy seasons.

Tamilnadu has a coastline of 1000 k.m. and salt has been produced since ancient times. Important salt producing centres in Tamilnadu are Thoothukudi and Vedaranyam. The other small salt producing units are located at Marakanam, Adirampatnam, Ramanathapuram, Nagercoil, etc. The average production per acre is 100 tones. There are more than 1000 salt manufacturing units both in the licensed and non-licensed sectors. The salt produced in their units is mostly consumed by salt-based industries in and outside the state. Of all the states, Gujarat comes first in production of salt. Tamilnadu ranks second in production of salt by contributing 14.75 per cent of the country's total output, which was 187 lakh tones in 2006.

Thoothkudi occupies a unique position in salt industries in India because of its geographic location and other favourable factors. Thoothukudi gets an uninterrupted manufacturing season of 9 to 10 months in a year as a result of long spell of dry water, low humidity, vast and flat land, impervious soil and protection from cyclones. An added advantage is that it has an even coastline, abundant supply of sunshine throughout the year and the availability of subsoil brine which is three to four times richer in salt content than sea water.

In Thoothukudi district, a great number of salt industries are at Mullakaddu, Thirespuram, Muthaiahpuram, Veplaodai, Pazhayakayal, Arumuganeri and Kayalpattnam. In these areas about 44000 adult workers both male and female are working. More than 100 salt industries are involved in producing salt. The salt industry in the study area is about 5000 acres. The salt production of the study area is approximately 50 lakhs tones per annum.

The unique character of the salt industry in that it is less capital-intensive and more employment-generating. It provides employment to a large number of skilled and unskilled workers. Workers are employed in *maramathu, watering, scraping, removing* and other types in the transport and distribution processes. Salt industry is dependant on salt workers.

Salt workers are casual workers, seasonal temporary workers, seasonal permanent workers and regular workers.

Casual workers are those employed for doing maramathu work in the beginning before the actual cultivation of salt in the beginning. They are paid daily wages. Seasonal temporary workers are employed temporarily during the harvest period. Some of them are paid daily and the others are paid weekly wages and are entitled to bonus.

Regular workers are those who are employed throughout the year. They are attached to the salt industry. They are not left free to work anywhere. They are paid monthly wages and entitled to bonus.

This present study includes all types of workers employed in the salt industries of Thoothukudi district. This industry plays a vital role in Tamilnadu's economy and it provides employment and a source of living to a very large number of people for whom there is no other alternative of livelihood. So, the researcher took up this study.

Objectives of the Study

The study has been carried out with the objectives to examine the following:

1. to know the nature of work and living condition of salt workers;
2. to find out the extent of exploitation of salt workers; and
3. to study the health problems of salt workers.

Operation Definition

Salt worker may be defined as work performed by male or female above 15 years of age relating to salt works with remuneration.

Methodology

The present study is an empirical one. Survey method was employed to collect the data from the salt workers. A well conceived and structural interview schedule was prepared and applied. The questions were based on the objectives of the study. To study the plight of salt workers in salt industries, 100 samples were selected. Here, the respondents were selected by convenient sampling method. Fieldwork for the present study was carried out personally by the researcher. The observation technique was applied to collect certain relevant data required for the study. Secondary data have also been collected from various books and journals.

Findings

In salt works both male and female workers are working. They are performing different types of work like maramathu work, watering, scraping, removing and others types of work. Of the total sample workers two-third are male workers and one-third are female workers.

Salt work is a hard and difficult task, heavy manpower and good physical strength are indispensable to do this work. As such it would be difficult, one has to take up this occupation at an early age and not able to continue with this occupation after sixty years. Of the total sample respondents, majority of them are in the age group of 20-30 years, one-third of them is in the age group of 30-40 years. One tenth of them are in the age group of 40-50 and another one-fifth of them are 50-60 years and very few are in the age of above 60 years. 20-30 years age group of male workers are normally involved in maramathu and scarping works. Female workers in the age group of 30-50 years are involved in watering and removing. 40-50 years age group of both male and female workers are involved in watering and other small works.

Three-fourths of the salt workers are Hindus and one-forth of them are Christians. No muslim workers are in salt industries.

A large majority of the salt workers in the area surveyed are married. Only one-tenth of them are unmarried. Most of the salt workers get early marriage due to their work environment and family situation.

Large family size of a majority of respondents is the serious problem in their households. As a result of the oversized families, the respondents find it difficult to meet even their basic needs for food, clothing and shelter. As they have to support their large families with their meagre income, they are unable to come out of the poverty cycle. It is clear from this study that the families of the majority respondents are really oversized (6-8) and it stands as an obstacle for the improvement of their living standards.

Education plays a vital role in transforming the cultural, social and political nature of any society. The right functioning of the society also demands the acceptance of a common knowledge, whether, it is a democracy state or a different one. Education contributes to human resource development which is the crux of development. The maximum level of education of salt workers is tenth standard. Of the total respondents, majority of them are illiterates. One-third of them have studied 1-5 Std., one-tenth have studied 6-8 Std. and very few have studied tenth Std. Salt workers are very backward in education. Most of the salt workers are illiterates. Their backwardness in this sphere may be attributed to several reasons like their traditional attitudes, cultural problems, Financial handicaps and the like.

It is found out during the survey that, though respondents themselves had little formal education, they are mostly aware of the need for education to their children. They have recognized the fact that those who have education are better of in the society and command social respect. The poor economic condition in many cases stands as an obstacle in educating their children. There are some reasons for not giving proper education to the children. With a view to supplement the income of the family, they send their children as coolies to work any where. Besides, the elder ones are retained at house to work with younger ones. However the awareness of education which they have, is very positive and is bound to grow in future.

Employment in salt industries is seasonal and intermittent. There is a heavy demand for workers in the middle of January for doing the *maramathu* work in the beginning of cultivation. Even child labourers are engaged for doing this work. When the actual cultivation work starts, the permanent workers alone will get employment. These workers will be thrown out of employment in the rainy season, that is, in October, November and December. Thus, the nature of employment is highly seasonal.

This means that the salt workers are mostly doing this work for eight to nine months in a year. In other words, they are without work in salt industries for three to four months in a year. During the off-seasons the female workers generally prefer to stay at home. Most of the male workers seek employment in construction work, road work and agricultural operations. This work is not regular and will not be available daily. They manage to get this work only for 12 to 15 days in a month. Incomes from this work provides a source of a supplemental income to the salt workers. However, it is by no mean certain or undesirable. Therefore, during the off seasons, these salt workers tend to fall back upon the small savings made during the eight to nine months of works in salt industry and borrow from the moneylender.

The saltworks include *maramathu, watering, scraping, removing* and other types of assisting work. In these works majority of the workers are female workers. Female workers are highly concentrating on *maramathu* and *removing*. Watering and *scraping* works are normally undertaken by male workers. Other types of assisting works are carried out by young male and female workers.

In the salt industries one-tenth of the workers are involved in *maramathu* works, majority of the workers are involved in *scraping*, one-third of the workers are involved in *removing* work and very few workers are involved in other types of assisting work.

The Factory's act lays down the rule that the workers should not work more than eight hours in a day or more than forty eight hours in a week. But in salt industries workers are working more than 10 hours in a day. Three-forth of the respondents are working 10-12 hours in a day one-fourth of the workers are working 8-10 hours. Thus it is identified that a large majority of the salt workers are working 10-12 hours. They have no weekly holiday. They are working in a very hot sunlight. They are doing their work from 8.00 a.m. to 6 p.m. They have only 15-30 minutes break for their lunch and other activities. Also they are in the salt fields moisturing their feet throughout the day.

Labour is one of the important factors of production. Wage is the price paid for labour services. In other words, wages are for work done by the workers. They exclude holiday pay, overtime pay, family allowances, bonus, etc. Salt industries are less capital-intensive but more employment-generating. About 44000 workers are engaged in salt industries of Thoothukudi district. These workers are paid wages regularly once in a week (or) fortnightly (or) monthly. But a majority of the workers are getting their wages weekly. The workers are not getting different components as basic wages, dearness allowance, House Rent Allowance, Medical Allowance, etc. They are not getting their wages as per payment of Wages Act, 1936. Minimum Wages Act, 1948 and Workmen's Compensation Act, 1923 in the study area. They are getting wages on the basis of their nature of the work. But in an average women workers are getting Rs. 75 per day and men workers are getting Rs. 100 per day. But, few workers are getting their wages on the basis of a fixed quantum of work during the working hours daily.

Since salt industry is highly an unorganized sector, the records relating to labour are not maintained properly. That is, Service Register of Workers, Time Cards, Pay Register etc.

The Minimum Wages Act was introduced in 1948. The objective of the Act is to protect the interest of the workers in a competitive market by fixing the minimum rates of wages in employments. The Act was made enforceable to salt industries in Tamilnadu from the year 1977. But in this study area, the workers are not paid the statutory minimum wage.

Since the salt workers are unemployed in salt industry for 3-4 months and they also do not get other alternative works in the off-season, subsistence allowance for retaining may be given to the salt workers during off-seasons for these periods.

In this study, the respondents expressed that all of them are not classified in the adequacy of the amount of existing wages. The workers feel that the existing rate of wage is inadequate. Because the workers are working for 8-12 hours in the hot sun light and moisturing their feet. So, adequate wages should be given. It should be reasonable and fair. At any cost it should not affect their mind. If they are paid reasonably, they would contribute their services whole-heartedly and happily.

The salt workers are paid a small amount of bonus. But all workers are not benefited, only few workers enjoy bonus benefit. The bonus fixation varies with nature of the work, work experience, sex, relationship with the employer, etc. Normally, Bonus is paid once in a year usually during the Deepavali/Christmas festival season. A majority of the employers distribute the bonus in cash and in kind like dhotis, sarees, shirt, towel, etc.

In salt industries, bonus is not distributed as per law. The minimum rate is 8.33 per cent according to law. But workers are paid in a lump sum money i.e., Rs. 1,000 or Rs. 1,500 or Rs. 2,000. Gifts are not given to all workers. They are given only for their well wishers. While distributing the bonus/gifts, there is a discrimination due to sex, colour and religion. Normally, women workers are discouraged by their employers in distribution of bonus or gift in salt industries. This social menace should be avoided.

According to Report of the International Labour Organization, the employer should provide healthy and congenial surroundings with amenities conducive to good health and high morale. Thus, welfare measures include housing, medical educational facilities, provisions of canteen, facilities for rest and recreation, co-operative societies, provision of sanitary accommodations, holidays with pay, social insurance measures including sickness, Provident Fund, gratuities, pension, etc.

In the study area, very few workers, are getting housing facility but the workers feel that housing facilities offered by the employers are not satisfactory and inadequate. Salt workers are not enjoying the benefits of medical facilities. As per the surveyed data, there is no provision of canteen in salt industries in the study area. According to the provisions of the Factories Act, 1948, every factory should provide safe drinking water for all workers employed in salt industries. But they are not given adequate drinking water facilities. Provision of separate urinals and latrines for men and women workers engaged in the productions of salt is also denied by the majority of the employers. Very few industries provide this facility. But it is not a good/adequate one.

The salt workers are not provided rest rooms and recreation facilities, Co-operative Societies facility, Group Insurance Facilities, gratuity and pension benefits. But very few industries are providing Provident Fund facilities and medical facilities.

Housing facilities sanitary facilities, education facilities to their children, drinking water facilities and other welfare measures should be provided without discrimination.

Salt workers may be provided subsidized food, coffee, snacks, etc. to the workers on the workplace.

The level of income is an important element as it determines mostly the standard of living, saving and investment. Income for salt workers depends on their types of work and number of working days. Wage is fixed on the basis of the nature of work and experience.

The salt workers are extracted more work but get less wage. So, they are exploited by the salt industry owners.

In the study area, majority of salt workers spend upto Rs. 10 per day for their own. The salt workers have to meet their household expenses like food, clothing, education, medical expenses, recreational etc. It is normally based on the size of the family. The salt workers' personal expenditure mainly consists of tea and refreshment. But male workers spend more money on smoking, liquor due to bad friendship. Ultimately they are not able to meet family expenses, then it leads to borrowing. Normally, salt workers borrow money from friends, relatives and local moneylenders.

But very few salt workers save money and deposit in any local bank or chit fund. But a great majority of the salt workers are not able to save money due to minimum savings.

The existing wage rate should be revised to cope up with the rising prices. The discrimination in payment of wages should be avoided. The Bonus Act, 1965 should be effectively implemented to prevent the discrimination in payment of bonus.

Occupational health hazards have been recently given more importance because of the increase in occupational disease. The occupation itself causes a variety of health problems. They are slow and generally accumulate in their effects. Sometime, occupational diseases are serious enough that might cause even death. In salt industry the workers suffer from four kinds of occupational diseases that is back pain, skin diseases, eye problem and urinary infection. It is observed that most of the workers are not using cooling glasses and chapels. They are exposed to hot sun throughout the day. So the salt workers are directly exposed to sodium chloride during the working hours, they are easily prone to health hazards. To start with they from them *'Photo phobia'* and *"Dimness of vision"*. Due to negligence on the part of workers and lack of good medical facilities they have to loose their eye sight in the long run. So, the owners should provide cooling glasses to all the workers.

The owners should also provide two pairs of chapels, canvas shoes, and rubber gloves. Because, the salt workers are in constant contract with salt throughout their working period, they are more prone to *'Tines'* a skin decease caused by fungus.

All the time, the salt workers are doing their work in standing position without taking rest and drinking water sufficiently. So, a large majority of the salt workers suffer from back pain and urinary infection.

In the study area majority of the women workers are affected by skin and back pain diseases. But majority of the men workers are affected by eye problem and back pain. Few male and female workers are affected by urinary infection. Sometimes it leads to kidney problem. But these occupational diseases attacking salt workers are found to be chronic.

For these occupational diseases only one-tenth of the workers are getting medical facilities from their employer. But their medical support is not adequate. Two-thirds of the salt workers are getting medical facilities from the government hospitals because they are not able to meet the medical expenses from their own. But one-fourth of them are getting medical facilities from private hospitals because the diseases are very acute. For their survival and saving their life they have to go to private hospitals to get necessary treatment. For which they are availing loan facilities from the local money lenders.

Salt industries are not providing medical facilities to the salt workers. So, salt workers are getting treatment from government hospital and the workers have to get off from work and it leads to lose wages for one day staying away from their work. Also, they are incurring additional expenditure in visiting hospital. Hence, the salt industry provides an adequate medical facility for their salt workers through Employees State Insurance medical scheme. Since, most of the salt workers are prone to occupational diseases, a separate hospital with all facilites should be established for the salt workers' benefit in Thoothukudi, through which thousands of salt workers can save their life.

Conclusion

Even though, the unorganized sector has been the most vulnerable and ignored sector in India, it holds an inevitable place in Indian economy. Thus, there is no exaggeration in saying that the backbone of Indian workforce is the unorganized sector and not the organized one.

Yet there is a tendency to ignore the vast mass of salt workers, as these thousands who belong to organized sector are politically powerless and economically weak. More than 60 per cent of the population of the country depends upon the earnings of the workers in an unorganized sector for their livelihood. In Thoothukudi District about 44,000 families depend upon this salt industry for their survival. Hence, there is an urgent need to give top priority to the issues and problems of the unorganized workers in salt industries.

REFERENCES

1. Banerjee, B., *"The Role of Informal Sector in the Migration Process: A Test of Probabilistic Migration Models and Labour Market Segmentation in India"*, in Oxford Economic Papers (Oxford University Press), 1983.
2. Das, Keshab, *"The Unorganised Sector"* in Alternative Survey Group, Alternative Economic Survey: 1991-1998, Rainbow Publishes Ltd. New Delhi, 1998.
3. Papola, T.S., *"Urban Informal Sector in a Developing Economy"*, Vikas Publishing House Pvt. Ltd., New Delhi. 1984.
4. Ramnath Sharma, *"Labour Problems, Social Security and Welfare"*, A Rajhana Publications, Meerut, 1996.
5. Ruddar Datt, *"Economic Reforms, Labour and Employment"*, Deep & Deep Publications, New Delhi, 2000.
6. Singh, D.P., *"Women Workers in Unorganised Sector,"* Deep & Deep Publications, New Delhi, 2005.
7. Subrahmanaya, R.K.A.,*"The Unorganised Sector: Work Security and Social Protections"*, Sage Publications, New Delhi, 2000.

10

A Study on Palmyrah Tappers in Thoothukudi District

Mrs. J. Shobana*

Introduction

India is one of the countries blessed with rich growth of palms. In India palmyrah trees are grown in the states of Tamilnadu, Andhra Pradesh, West Bengal, Kerala and Mysore. They are widely planted in the district of Coimbatore, Kanyakumari, Tirunelveli, Thoothukudi, Thiruchirapalli and Ramanathapuram in Tamilnadu. The Khadi and Village Industries Commission classified palmyrah industry as one of the important village industries in India. Palmyrah juice is not only a good liquid food but is an excellent food for typhoid both at an early as well advanced stages. Jaggery contains chemicals like Calcium and Phosphorous which is good for health.

Palms produced a sweet sap, neera in abundance. People turned to these palms in hope of making a living, since their options were limited in the absence of suitable employment avenues. Jaggery is used as sugar. However it did not bring sweetness to the lives of the tappers. Instead the tappers and their

* **M.Com., M.Phil., Lecturer, Vidyasagar College of Arts and Science, Udumalpet – 642 126, Tamilnadu.**

families experienced misery and sorrow. Children were laboured with their parents for their daily bread. Schools were out of the reach of boys and girls. Boiling neera required not only the labour of the tappers, but the entire family.

The work of a tapper starts in the morning with the climbing of trees for tapping neera, bringing the neera from different places to the house, boiling it to convert it into Jaggery. Not only the tapper but also the whole members of the family have to engage in this occupation. The palmyrah tappers and their family are backward in Education. Proper and alternative employment is not available to the palmyrah tappers in the off-season. They cannot meet even their basic requirements of food, clothing and shelter because of their low income. Most of them live in thatched huts without proper sanitary, lighting and drinking water facilities.

In the Bible, there is a simple but beautiful parable of a seed. The seed falls to the ground, covered by the dust, then sprouts and stretches forth its branches to give shelter to many birds. In the same way, one can say that here is the parable of the palmyrah nut, despised, disregarded, discarded and thrown into the dust, only to sprout as a hardy and formidable palmyrah palm that will shelter the downtrodden of our society.

"Neera can be converted into Jaggery, sweet as honey itself. This jaggery is superior to cane jaggery, Cane jaggery is sweet but palm jeggery is sweet and delicious; it can be produced worth crores of rupees. Palmgur gives mineral salt too. Where there are the way of banishing poverty from our land. This is an antidote to Poverty.

—Mahathma Gandhi

The palm is described as the "Princess of the vegetable Kingdom" in the British Encyclopedia. The family of palm constitutes nearly 1,100 species, widely scattered over the world with their concentration in tropical countries. However only 9 species yield sweet juice known as Neera, the basic raw material for the manufacture of jaggery, sugar and candy besides its direct consumption as a health beverage.

Objectives of the Study

The basic objectives of the study is to learn about the palmyrah tappers. The study focus on the following specific objectives.

1. To study about the History of Palmyrah Tappers.
2. To examine about the palm wealth.
3. To analyze the socio-economic condition of the Palmyrah Tappers in Thoothukudi District.
4. To examine the various problems faced by the Palmyrah Tappers with regard to production and marketing of Jaggery.

Statement of the Problem

Despite the various welfare measures taken by the Government, majority of Palmyrah Tappers in Thoothukudi district live in utmost poverty. They are the outliers of mainstream development process. Housing, sanitation and drinking water facilities are highly inadequate. The literacy rate is too low. This poor standard of living resembles the stonage or tribal culture. So the socio-economic cultural backwardness of Thoothukudi district Palmyarh Tappers should be analyzed from an entirely different angle, that is, from the point of view of their income and expenditure pattern which among other factors plays a vital role in the lives of Palmyarh Tappers.

Down the ages, the needs of the Palmyrah workers have remained unfulfilled. The development activities initiated by the government through Primary Jaggery Manufacturing Societies and the District Federations have failed to effect adequate advancements in the socio-economic life of the artisans. The overall measures undertaken for the development by-passed the weaker sections. The organized and the pressure groups were even able to turn the national policies in their favour. In spite of all efforts for socio-economic reforms, the basic systems and cultural values refuse to undergo change in the manner desired. Therefore such efforts need to be supplemented by the efforts of voluntary organization. The present study is a maiden attempt to highlight the impact of this society on the Palmyrah workers.

Palmyrah Tappers

Tapping is both a difficult and hazardous job. A young and healthy tapper can climb usually 40 to 50 palms twice a day. In the early hours of the day, at around 5 o'clock, tappers start climbing palms for collecting the neera dripped into the *kalasam* (pot). It will last until noon. Again, in the afternoon, at around 3 o'clock, they ascend the palms for the second time. This time it is to cut and prepare the inflorescence for the next day. This work may continue right into the night. Once neera is collected and brought down, it has to be processed to be converted into jaggery (*karupetty*). This process involves considerable human labour. The labour of the whole family is required at this stage. The tapper's wife and children then take charge of processing neera. Boiling neera requires hours of work. First, firewood has to be procured, often by trekking long distances. Women and children in the family stay close to the fireplace, watching the boiling of neera in the earthen pans to the level required to form jaggery. To produce one kg of jaggery, eight litres of neera are to be boiled. When the final product is ready, they then carry it head-load to the local market, and return with the things for the day's consumption. The price they fetch for their product is hardly enough for meeting the family's daily needs. The price of the jaggery is invariably determined by the merchants, mostly from Kottayam and Chennai. Forced to sell the product at the price dictated by the traders, the producers have remained an exploited group. Satisfying themselves usually with tapioca and rarely with rice, the tapper's family carries on, for, they have no other option. Gainful employments other than this are rather limited. Due to the dangerous nature of the job, accident rates are high among tappers. Some workers sustain serious injuries, which prevent them from returning to work. Very grave injuries may result in the workers being permanently bed-ridden, or worse, death. A fatal injury hits the already poor family the hardest.

The Nadars, also called Shanars, were known for their association with palmyrah palms. In the beginning of the nineteenth century, almost the entire population of Nadars were engaged either in the cultivation or climbing of palms. In the early years of the Twentieth century, the Nadars were numerically strong in the areas to the south of the Tamraparni river extending to Kanyakumari (Pate, 1917: 496). About eighty to ninety per cent of the total population in the Palmyrah forests of the Tiruchendur were Nadars. The Nadars are believed to have migrated from the northern coast of Sri Lanka and entered Tirunelvely in Tamilnadu via Ramnad (Caldwell, 1849: 4-5). Along with them, they brought the seeds of Jaffna Palmyrah. Later, on their arrival in Tamilnadu, the Pandyan rulers granted them the title over the sandy wastelands which were found to be suitable for the cultivation of Palmyrah palms. As Palmyrah-climbers and toddy-tappers, the Nadars suffered severe social disabilities (Hardgrave, 1969: vii). The landed gentry in the area, namely the Nayars, oppressed the Nadar community in a number of ways, often engaging the members of the community as servants. In the southern parts of Travancore (now part of Kerala) and in the eastern areas of Kanyakumari and towards the west, the Palmyrah climbers were subtenants to powerful Nayar landlords. In the areas bordering Tirunelvely District, they were subtenants to the Vellala landlords.

Socially and economically the Nadars were a disadvantaged social group. Within the community there were a number of divisions. Broadly, the division between the palmyrah-climbers and the palmyrah-owners was clear, segregating them into two separate socioeconomic categories. The palmyrah-climbers formed the most neglected and backward segment. They remained one of the most economically depressed communities in Tamilnadu (Hardgrave, 1969: vii). Tapping was not recognized as a dignified occupation then and hence within the community the tappers could not enjoy a status equivalent to that of the non-tappers. The trading Nadars, who were economically well-off, were common in Virudhnagar and Satur areas of Tamilnadu. The barren Palmyrah forests in Tiruchendur were owned by Nadars, but the majority of the climbers were landless (Hardgrave, 1969: 28).

The Jesuits working among the Pearl fishers of Thoothukudi were among the first missionaries who encountered the Nadars. There were other missionary congregations such as the London Missionary Society and Anglican missionaries as well. Around the year 1841, there was a 'mass movement' among the Nadars to embrace Christianity, not as single individuals or families but as whole villages (Hardgrave, 1969: 46) and this happened primarily among the Palmyrah climbers. The missionary records reveal that the Shanars were more inclined to embrace Christianity than any other native castes. For the community, conversion to Christianity was a means to improve their position, both social and economic. A study done in Tirunelvely district in 1941 showed that about forty per cent of the Nadars in the district were engaged in tapping, but the per cent was only twenty among the Christian Nadar. Nadars in Tiruchendur Taluk and in the Palmyrah forests of southeastern Tirunelvely district were doing the job of jaggery-making while in the other regions of Tirunelvely and to the north they were mostly engaged in tapping, distribution and sale of toddy (Hardgrave, 1969: 137).

Palm Wealth

Since 1986, scientific education development for community development (SEDCO) at Sathankulam in Thoothukudi District, is engaged in conservation and development activities of natural resources. Estimation of palm wealth in India, as done by the Khadi and Village Industries, shows that there were 102 million palms in 1986, of which 69 million were tappable. But only 12.3 million (12.06%) palms were made use of for tapping purpose. In Tamilnadu, referring to the same period, there were 51.9 million palms of which 35.3 million were tappable i.e., 70 per cent. Here again, only a small portion of them, say 11.8 million (32.5% of the tappable palms), were used for tapping, supporting a population of 0.569 million artisans. Palmyrah (*Borassus flabellifer*) is native of Tropical Africa. Borassus is a genus of four species and *B. Flabellifer* is the only species found in India. It is found in many dry parts of India, Myanmar, Sri Lanka and Malaysia. The palms grow to a height of about 40 to 60 feet, and sometimes as tall as a hundred feet, with a girth of 3.5 to 7 feet. It is one of the palms which produce a sweet sap called neera, or sweet toddy, a nutritious beverage. (Other sap producing palms include *Caryota urens, Cocos nucifera, Nipa fruticans* and *Phoenix sylvestris*). The sap is being used as a stimulant and antiphelgmatice and for inflammatory affections and dropsy

One tree gives approximately 0.5 gallon (2.25 litres) neera a day during the season, but it varies from month to month. A particular season and its duration varies from place to place within the same state. The yield of neera will be more during winter. As well, there are male and female palms and the later produces relatively more neera. Male tree produces only two-thirds of a female tree can produce. When a tree is 25 to 30 years old, it is ready for tapping and it will yield for about 30 years. In some places, tapping begins around the 15th year. Every three years, the trees are left to recover. It is the Kalpa tree, the Hindu tree of life, and one among the five trees of the Hindu paradise that is used for tapping (Quoted in Hardgrave, 1969: 25). The Tamil poet Arunachalam speaks of 801 uses of Palmyrah. Palm gur (*Karupetty*) palm candy (*Panam Kalkkandu*) are other major products made from neera. The Tamil proverb is that the tree lives a thousand years and it lasts another thousand years which it dies. It is the only palm whose wood is valuable, its roots and fruits are edible and leaves are used for thatching houses, and for making handicraft articles. Annually, a palm can, on average produce 150 litres of neera, one kg. fibre, 1.5 kg. eark and eight leaves. Out of this, one can make 24 kg. gur, two baskets, two brush and six mats.

Climbing the palm, tapping, too, is a hard job. In male trees, the flowering shoots are bruised using wooden sticks called *Kadippu*. Once it is bruised, two or three days later in the evening, it is scraped and the tips are pared off with the tapping knife (*katthi*). Throughout the night, neera will be collected drop by drop into a small earthen pottied to the stalk. In the case of female palms, the inflorescence is cut when the nuts are very small, but only the tips are squeezed, beaten and pared off. Palmyrah juice is a good liquid food. Though climbing is not liked by all people, the demand for palmyrah juice and the final product called jaggery is universal. It is very useful and is part of the regular diet of a considerable number of people.

The composition of palmyrah gur is as follows (in per cent).

1.	Moisture	8.61
2.	Sucrose	76.86
3.	Reducing Sugar	1.48
4.	Fats	0.19
5.	Proteins	1.04
6.	Total minerals	3.15
7.	Calcium as Cao	0.86
8.	Phosphorus as P 205	0.052

The nutritive values of palm gur are given below based on an analysis (out of 100 Gms) of the Nutritional Research Laboratories, Indian Council of Medical Research.

1.	Thiamine (Vit. B)	21 mgm
2.	Ribofiavin (Vit. B)	432 mgm
3.	Nicotinic Acid (Antipallagra Vitamin)	5.24 mgm
4.	Ascorbic Acid (Vit. C)	11 mgm

Source: "Wealth from the Palms" p. 9.

The cost structure of Palmyrah gur as worked out while conducting palm gur price fixation enquiry is as follows. (in per cent)

1.	Tree rent	15
2.	Fuel	11
3.	Chemicals	2
4.	Depreciation	7
5.	Overheads	4
6.	Earnings	61

Source: Wealth from the Palms, p. 17.

Jaggery has long been known in India. The liquor extracted from the Palmyrah tree is converted into a black rock of sugar called jaggery. Jaggery contains chemicals like calcium and phosphorous. Jaggery is generally prepared and consumed in the states of Tamilnadu, Andhra Pradesh, Bengal, Mysore and Kerala. Kerala tops in the list of maximum consumption of jaggery.

Palm Candy and Sugar

Palm Candy, *Panam Kalkkandu* in local parlance, is a Crystalline form of sucrose contained in neera. Neera is first heated to 40°-60°C in order to remove its impurities. It is then delimed to bring the pH around 8, and filtered to remove the sediments. Again, it is boiled up to 108°C when it turns into a syrup form. This syrup is then transferred to a specially made container, crystallizer, and kept intact for 41 days. During this period, the syrup undergoes a process of crystallization and pearl-like candy crystals grow in the crystallizer. The remaining molasses in the crystallizer is again boiled at 108°C to repeat the same process. The crystals can be harvested on the 41st day. They are to be washed and dried in the sun before packing. On the basis of the color and size, candy is graded into five categories of export quality, Parumani, Salankai, Saral and Podisaral.

Palm Candy is manufactured from boiled neera. It is widely used for medicinal purposes as well as for other domestic uses. Making palm candy is a traditional art of Tamilnadu. A training centre has been started at Tiruchendur, Tuticorin District by the state Federation to impart training in the manufacture of palm candy by using improved techniques. As the neera in Tiruchendur area contains more sucrose than elsewhere, the centre is efficiently run at Tiruchendur with an annual production of one ton of candy.

Fibre

It is one of the important by-products of the industry extracting fibre from the Palmyrah tree. During the months of April, May and June the artisans engage in fibre making. A variety of articles like brushes, foot rugs and mats are manufactured out of fibre. The Tamilnadu State Palmgur Federation has an export wing in Colachel with branches at Thoothukudi, dealing with fibre export trade. Palmyrah fibre has, today, great export potential and earning about two crores in foreign exchange annually.

Palmyrah Leaf *Eark* and *Naar*

A variety of fancy and utility articles can be made from palmyrah leaf and its mid-rib called *eark*. Articles like fans, bags, mats, wall mats and many other decorative articles are made out of leaves. Artistic and beautifully made Palmyrah leaf articles are in great demand both in our country and abroad. A unit was started by the Tamilnadu State Palmgur Co-operative Federation in 1974 at Meignanapuram in Thoothukudi District. Nearly 125 persons are employed of which 50 have studied upto S.S.L.C. They are trained in the manufacture of leaf articles like fans, garlands, tablemats etc. Also, a Palm Leaf Co-operative Industrial Society, functioning at Manapad, is helping the fisher-women to utilize their spare time profitably and supplement their income. The goods are exported mainly to London.

The word *'naar'* originated from Tamil language. Outer and inner skins of the petiole are known as *agani* and *putani* respectively. It is used for making baskets of different shapes, mats, cots, and chairs. Even the waste fibrous material is coloured and made into mats. It is carried out as a household industry in Tamilnadu.

Social Life and Awareness of Palmyrah Tappers

Health and hygiene is one of the main problems the Palmyrah workers are faced with. No one can say that the Palmyrah workers are poor in physical health. But the physical health of their wives and children is deplorable. Poor sanitation and unhygienic diets contribute to their health problem. Primarily, they live in poorly-built houses with one or two rooms—one of which may be used as Kitchen. Since there is no chimney as such provided for the outlet of smoke, which is dense since dry leaves and cashew-shells are used as substitutes for firewood for converting juice into jaggery, the entire soot settles on the unplastered walls and is inhaled by the poor wives and children of the artisans who are engaged in the processing. Moreover, the process of making jaggery being still in its primitive forms, the entire household of the worker is involved in the work. Since the whole day is spent in processing, the wives and children find no time even for a bath and as the workers do not have spacious courtyard and backyard, they dump all their filthy rags and rubbish either in front or back of the house. They are thus vulnerable to all kinds of diseases. Many mothers find no time to bath or clean their children. Malnutrition is the cause of children's diseases. In short, they suffer much due to lack of knowledge of sanitation and hygiene.

Development is not primarily a function of economic growth. It is a complex process of human progress. Even if rapid growth is experienced, the social life, awareness and social structure may, remain unaffected. There must be a radical change in the mentality of the people. The social and cultural life of the workers are dis-heartening. They have little social life or enjoyments. It does not mean that they are unaware of their wants in their respect. Due to the prevailing situation they are forced not to think on progressive lines but to keep to traditional modes. One cannot even imagine the situations in which the children of most of the tappers are brought up. They are ill-clad and poorly fed. The social life of a relatively small section of workers (who are well-placed economically and literally amongst workers) alone seems to be satisfactory, when compared with the vast majority of workers.

Some of the workers are reacting against some aspects of the traditional society which hampers development. This is particularly found among the young tappers and the youth in the tapper families. Such an awareness is bound to grow in future and is a healthy sign of change and development.

Family size greatly influences the standard of life of a household directly as well as indirectly. Though the large size of their families leads to a low level of per capita income and consumption stands, they do not seem to be worried about it. It reveals that they are still traditional in their level of thinking. Generally most of the people are ignorant of family planning. It is their conviction that children are the gift of God. It is one of the important problems of the workers.

Jaggery manufacturing requires boiling of the juice for a number of hours in order to evaporate the water. Their firewood requirements are generally met by the local retail merchants and neighbours too by paying exhorbitant rates. Dry leaves etc. are used for this purpose but it serves to solve only a part of the problem of fuel consumption. It can be seen that the children of these workers go to the nearest forests or to the dense groves to collect dry leaves and dry wood. It also partly helps them to reduce their expenditure on fuel. The firewood problem really needs adequate attention. It is a problem faced by a vast majority of the households. The problems of unemployment and underemployment for the tappers throughout the year and the same problem of unemployment in their households really stand as obstacles in their growth. Some of the problems of unemployment and underemployment are:

- Scarcity of workers.
- Scarcity of trees.
- Lack of storage and preservation.
- Lack of adequate scientific research in the industry
- Lack of adequate efforts at the government level for the development of the industry and improving the lot of the workers.
- The by-products of the industry are not effectively utilized so far.
- Adequate efforts are not taken for marketing of products within and outside the country and so on.

PROBLEMS OF PALMYRAH TAPPERS

Problem in Production of Jaggery

The neera kept in the pan will have to be boiled to make a more profitable product then jaggery value-added product is the panam which means *kalkkandu* (palm candy). The production of jaggery is experienced to be, for more than one reason, an economically non-profitable activity. The processing of neera into jaggery is labour-intensive and consumes expensive and scarce firewood. Women and children in the family were left with the task of boiling neera for hours together. On this account, children would have to skip their classes often from the school. They had to do errands in this connection: carrying firewood, keeping the fire in the *choola* alive while neera was boiled, looking after the younger ones when parents were away at work and taking jaggery to the market were part of the children's job when their families were engaged in jaggery production. Considering the extent of the risk in collection of neera and the labour involved in processing, monetary benefits were rather insignificant. More often than not, the producers were able to make only a paltry sum from their produce. Middlemen, moneylenders and the market forces acted against palmyrah workers. Although PWDS in the beginning helped the workers by getting them firewood, disbursing small loans and intervening in the market for securing a fair price for the produce, a better strategy was being planned.

Team for income generation and product promotion support, called TIPS, was thus born to motivate the palmyrah workers to start candy making units and direct them to similar income-generating activities. TIPS extended support and requisite training inputs to set up candy making units as a group enterprise. Marketing responsibilities, too were shouldered by TIPS. TIPS, on its part, makes palmyrah workers aware of the advantages of candy making and the profit it can bring in for them. Tapper leaders including women are trained in the production of candy. Followed by this, TIPS, helps the unit in mobilizing financial resources, constructing the *choolah* and marketing the product. TIPS then steps in to provide training. The group should be able to supply a minimum of 400 litres of neera everyday, during the season. The members will be paid Re.1 as an advance for every litre of neera they supply to the unit. When the product is sold the members get their share of the profit the unit could make.

Problems in Marketing of Jaggery

Marketing is the crux of all our problems related to both agriculture and industry. The marketing of jaggery is not only defective but also the entire system is deplorable. Because of the unsound financial position of the tappers, they are forced to sell their products at low prices, without waiting to get a higher price. Due to the low preserving capacity of the products, it cannot enjoy a good reputation in the national and international markets. Lack of market intelligence is a major problem faced by the tappers in marketing. The non-availability of up-to-date information and the ignorance of the tappers make them believe whatever the trader tells about the prices.

Marketing is one of the chronic problem, the cottage and village industries are facing today. The marketing of jaggery possess tremendous problems. Most of the tappers have to sell their products at an unfavourable place, at an unfavourable time and on unfavourable terms. There are two methods for marketing of jaggery. The first and the most common method is to sell jaggery at the village level. The urgent need for money, ignorance about market prices and lack of time to go to the market, compel the tappers to sell their products at the village level. Since the workers sell a substantial portion of their products at the village level, it naturally leads to an intervention by a number of middlemen. The second method of selling jaggery is at the markets in towns which may be either daily or weekly.

A large majority of the tappers and their families lived in small thatched huts, hardly enough to lodge all the members under the roof. The huts were not spacious enough to provide the minimum basic requirement of space for their dwellers. Moreover, these huts were not a safe place for living, especially for those who made jaggery at home. Boiling neera in the open fire-place posed threat to the huts which are made up of wood and leaves of the palmyrah palms. Incidents of fire accident were not few and far between. Erecting a hut and building up the life again from scratch is not an easy affair for the poor palmyrah workers. Fire accidents, for the palmyrah workers, have been a perennial problem which is invariably coupled with jaggery making. The solution to this problem is either to abstain from jaggery making or to have a pucka house which can prevent fire accidents. The Palmyrah tappers request ten demands to the Government at times of accidents, facilities for health, housing and education, and better price for their products.

TEN DEMANDS

1. Set up a separate corporation for the production of palm-based products.
2. As Government land leased out to people, lease palms to palmyrah workers.
3. For the Government, remit the insurance premium for the palmyrah workers.
4. Give pension to palmyrah workers when they are no longer able to do the job.
5. Undertake scientific research to diversify the use of palmyrah products.
6. For the Government, establish a support price for jaggery.
7. Give special consideration to tapper families for education, health, housing and employment.

8. Sanction an ex gratia amount before doing postmortems in the case of deaths resulting from falls from palm trees.

9. Give Rs. 15,000 to the families of the men killed in accidents while working in the palmyrahs and Rs. 7,500 to those who can no longer climb as a result of accidents.

10. For the Government, route the loan schemes and other programmes through the organization of palmyrah workers (PWDS—Palmyrah Workers Development Society)

Findings

1. The Nadars also called Shanars were known for their association with palmyrah palms. About eighty to ninety per cent of the total population in the palmyrah forests of the Tiruchendur were Nadars. The Jesuits working among the Pearl fishers of the Tuticorin were among the first missionaries who encountered the Nadars.

2. Since 1986, Scientific Education Development for community development (SEDCO) at Sathankulam in Thoothukudi District, is engaged in conservation and development activities of natural resources.

3. The palmyrah workers are economically very poor. With their meagre income they cannot afford to maintain a high standard of living.

4. The people of the other sections of the society do not like to mingle with this poor group and they themselves hesitate to mingle with other. The difficulty they face on the matter of marriages of their children reflects how this poor group is isolated from the other sections of the society.

5. The palmyrah tappers and their family are backward in education also. Insufficient income is the main cause for not giving proper and higher education to their children. Another reason for not sending the children to schools is that the assistance of the children is needed in helping the parents to collect firewood, to boil neera and to look after the younger ones at homes.

6. They cannot meet even their basic requirements of food, clothing and shelter because of their low income. Most of them live in thatched huts without proper sanitary, lighting and drinking water facilities.

7. The work involves a series of difficult process. The work of a tapper starts in the morning with the climbing of trees for tapping neera, bringing the neera from different places to the house, boiling it to convert it into jaggery and marketing of jaggery. Not only the tapper but also other members of the family have to engage in this occupation. Thus though the job is a tedious one it is not properly rewarded.

8. The job is of a risky nature. Tapping is a very hazardous occupation leading to permanent disability and deaths following accidents. But proper relief is not given to the affected family against the risk with a view to support them financially.

9. The boiling of neera for its being conversion into jaggery requires large quantity of firewood. A serious problem faced by the tappers is the procurement of firewood at the proper times. Considering the rising prices of firewood, the price available for jaggery in the market is very low.

10. Tappers are subject to heavy exploitation in the markets by the middlemen. The urgent need for money compel them to sell the jaggery every day. They cannot store their product and cannot take advantage of higher prices in the off-season. Knowing their urgency for money, the middlemen are exploiting them. They lend money to them and absorb their entire output at a reduced rate.

REFERENCES

1. Sambandhan, "Palmyrah Industry" *Tad Gud Samachar*, Khadi Village Industries Commission, Murtri Bhavan, Dinshaw Watch Road, Bombay, July 1958, p. 267.

2. Khadi and Village Industries Commission, "Wealth from the Palms". 1975.

3. B.R. "Palmyrah Palm Speaks", *Souvenir*, Khadi and Village Industries Commission, Gramodaya 3, Irla Road, Vile Parie (W) Bombay, 1987.

4. R. Soorymoorthy "Climbing Up" The Story of Palmyrah Workers Development Society, PWDS, Marthandam, Year 2000.

5. See Robert Caldwell, "Report of the Edeiyengoody District for the Year Ending 30 June 1845", (Manuscript), Quoted in Hardgrave, 1969, p. 48.
6. Gnanadasan, Joy. 1994. *A Forgotten History: The Story of the Missionary Movement and the Liberation of People in South Travancore,* Gurukul Lutheran Theological College and Research Institute, Madras.
7. Bell, Evangeline Sheela. 1991. "History of the Palmyrah Worker's Development Society, Martandam, 1977-1990", Unpublished M.Phil Thesis submitted to Madurai Kamaraj University, Madurai.

Child Labour in India

A Study Towards Policy Intervention

Dr. G. Karunanithi*

Abstract

Child labour is not only a formidable threat to the Human Rights, but also a universal social problem, which needs to be approached from the social disorganisation perspective. An attempt to study the problem in India from this theoretical perspective would give a clear understanding of the relationship between the persistent economic pursuits of child labour on the one hand and their hand. This would also facilitate the understanding of the relationship between the demand and supply to child labour in the employment market associated with the unorganised sectors elsewhere in India. Further it would help to identify the relationship between this problem and education i.e. the absence of compulsory primary education in India would multiply the population of child labour. Moreover it would also open avenues to study as how does an alarming proportion of child labour in India lead the families supplying child labour to endless poverty? How does it disorganise

* **Professor and Head, Department of Sociology, Manonmaniam Sundaranar University Tirunelveli – 627 012, Tamilnadu, India.** ***E-mail:*** **karunanithig@gmail.com Mobile: 09442557750 Fax: 0462 – 2322973.**

such families at one point of time? And how does it ultimately result in social disorganisation of a sizeable section of population in Indian society as well.

While focusing the structural aspects of Indian society, this perspective would also explain the problem by referring to caste status. A major agenda of this perspective employed in this study is to refocus the intervention of Government and the NGOs in the task of eradicating this problem. An attempt is also made in the study to formulate critically the policy of intervention strategies of the Local Administration and the Non-Government Organisations. To study the problem in order to combat the problem of child labour altogether.

Introduction

Child labour is a universal problem challenging the Human Rights. It has aroused the public consciousness in contemporary India as it has been a serious issue in many of the Third World Countries. In India, about 17.5 million children below the age of 15 years are estimated to fall under the definition of child labour. A majority of them are from low caste groups including Scheduled Castes and Scheduled Tribes. Their population varies across states, but the proportion of working girls at national level is higher than the proportion of working boys. Besides helping their parents in their work, the children are engaged in various jobs mostly in unorganised sectors such as match, coir, carpet, lock, beedi[1] and the like. Some of them are identified as hazardous.

In India, there are about 370 million children below the age of 14 years and they constitute one-third of the total population of India. Of them, 120 to 170 millions are engaged in various types of work and of them, about 10 million children are bonded workers. Out of the total number of child workers, 80-90 per cent of them are domestic workers.[2]

Like other states in India, Tamilnadu has also been confronting the problem of child labour over decades. It is estimated that nearly two million children are working in Tamilnadu. They contribute over 6 per cent of workforce to the total child workforce in India. Besides, it is also estimated that the total main workers in Tamilnadu constitute over 5 per cent of the main child workers. The male main child workers account for nearly 4 per cent of the total male main workers, whereas the female main child workers account for more than 7 per cent of the total female main workers.[3]

Beedi making has been one of the primary occupations for a large number of families in certain districts of Tamilnadu. But, it is mainly concentrated in Tirunelveli and Vellore districts. In Tirunelveli district, over 90 per cent of the workforce engaged in beedi making, are women and girls who are basically home workers. The children work both as part time and full time workers. On the other hand, in Vellore district, a considerable number of men are engaged in this work with a large number of women and children. Besides, it is observed that a peculiar practice of pledging the children to the contractors of beedi units has been in vogue in the district over several decades. But, it is not found in Tirunelveli districts as well.

Methodology

This paper aims at study the plight of pledged children in the beedi units in a northern district (Vellore district) and the children engaged in the same work with their mothers in domestic settings in a southern district (Tirunelveli district) of Tamilnadu. The discussions in the paper are based on the data collected from a sample of 500 pledged children (246 girls and 254 boys) drawn from Vellore district during 1991-92 and a sample of 1000 children (909 girls and 91 boys) drawn from Tirunelveli district during 1994-95. All of them are in the age group of 8-14 years. They were selected on the basis of multistage sampling method. An Interview Schedule was administered to collect data from the parents of pledged children. In addition to this, two sets of Interview Guides were used to elicit data from the contractors of beedi units and pledged children. In order to gain more insights on the problems of those children, Observation and Case Study methods were also used in certain situations.

Discussion

Before taking up the main problem for discussion, it is relevant here to trace out the origin of the practice of pledging the children to the employers of beedi units in Vellore district. The study identifies two different views in this regard. One view is that a severe drought in the district after 1970 pushed several thousands of agrarian families into beedi making. As the drought continued for several years, a majority of landless agricultural workers developed an interest in this work as it was picking-up well. They continued this work hopefully to earn more than what they were earning from agricultural work. They also believed that this would bring them and their children a better future. However, contrary to their expectations, their earning was not adequate to meet the needs of their family members. So, at times, they mortgaged or sold much of their household and other valuable articles to feed their family members. When they had nothing left to mortgage or sell, they were forced to borrow money from the owners of beedi companies at times of exigencies. The labourers who were unable to repay the money, attached (bonded) themselves to their employees in order to compensate the debt.

Some parents used to put their children to work in beedi companies situated in their place. In course of time, as the employers found it profitable, they readily employed a large number of children just by advancing some loans to their parents. The obvious reason was that much labour can be extracted from the children for a low wage. This situation coupled with poverty, warranted the parents to pledge their children for want of money. After sometimes, the poor parents responded positively to the employers' requirements. Consequently this practice became popular in several parts of the district. It is clear from this that the employers were waiting for their turn to grab the chance of employing cheap labour. Thus, the employers' immediate supply of money to the needy parents perpetuated the pledging system in the district.

The other view is that the wide spread of contractor system itself accounts for the genesis of pledging system in beedi making in the district. When the Central and State Governments started pressurizing the owners of registered beedi factories to conform to the factory and labour laws, they modified the mode of production by introducing the contractor system in order to escape from the eyes of the laws. Under this system, the owners gave job works to the contractors who in turn supplied the owners with finished beedis. In the system, the adult beedi workers were located with unreasonable work norms. They were unable to complete the target of 5000 beedis per day fixed by the contractors. As a result, they put their children to work in order to assist them to complete the target. This decreased their workload but increased the responsibilities of their children. They consider their children as economic assets and therefore put them to work to make substantial contribution to the family income. According to them, earning is better than learning. That is perhaps the reason why most of them denied their children their right to education and play by putting heavy workload on their tender shoulders. It has resulted in pledging their children to the contractors for money. This has almost become a common practice among the families engaged in this work.

Even the parents having only one child want to do so not minding the future of the child. For instance, at the time of field work, over 15 per cent of the parents had one child each and surprisingly all these children were pledged. Besides, it is heart-rending to notice that nearly 50 per cent of the total number of children (1337) from a sample of 500 households was pledged to the contractors. The others are not pledged but full time beedi workers (10%), school going children but part-time beedi workers (5%), school going children who do not do this work (15%) and those below the age of 5 years (20%). However, of the total number of pledged children, the girls (about 55%) outnumber the boys (about 45%).

The study discloses that more number of girls (68.70%) than boys (51.18%) were pledged during their early childhood because of socio-cultural reason that the parents do not want to pledge their girls after puberty. The other reason is that the girls are more accommodative and adjustable than the boys are. On the contrary, the boys are brought into the system of pledging much later. This differences has resulted in the difference with regard to the educational levels of boys and girls. In other words, the proportion of literate boys is higher than the proportion of literate girls.

On the other hand, of the sample population drawn from Tirunelveli district, the proportion of girls (91%) is ten times as much as the proportion (9%) of boys. This can perhaps be explained in terms of the sex discrimination over centuries. It is observed during the survey that most of the parents do not force their boys to attend to beedi works even if they are reluctant to go to schools. They seem to be disinterested in training their sons to acquire the skill in the work in order to make them full-fledged beedi workers in future. They wish that their boys have to secure some jobs other than this work. It is, to them, not a decent job to men as well as boys.

In Vellore district, like the Scheduled Caste people (Ex-untouchables) and Most Backward Caste people (mostly landless agricultural labourers) are engaged in beedi-work. A similar employment situation in this sector is prevalent in Tirunelveli district. Besides, a sizeable section of backward caste people, especially the Nadars (mostly farmers and traders) and the Konars (mostly farmers and shepherds) do the work. This shows that those in the lower caste groups, in one way or other, are associated with jobs which the higher caste groups consider menial.

However, a large number of Muslims in both the sample districts are also engaged in the work. Normally they prefer jobs associated with handicrafts such as beedi, mat and carpet making. Nevertheless, it has been a traditional practice among the Muslim women that they mostly confine themselves to their homes and hardly make their presence in public places. Since the beedi making is one of the money making home-based jobs, they readily opted for it. In thousands of poor Muslim families, the women and girls are more potential and productive beedi workers than their male counterparts.

The average size of households with pledged children in Vellore District (6.85%) is relatively higher than the average size of households without pledged children in Tirunelveli district (5.97%). The average number of children per household in the former district is worked out to 2.6 per cent, whereas it is 3.4 per cent for the latter district. This leads to a conclusion that though the size of sample households are relatively larger than the size of households in Tamilnadu (4.47%), the couples in them seem to have not followed small family norm in spite of intensive family planning drive by the Government of India.

The survey conducted in Vellore district shows that the proportion of illiterate girls (59.35%) to the total number of sample girls is higher than the proportion of illiterate boys (54.72%) to the total number of sample boys. Nevertheless, almost similar proportions of boys (35.83%) and girls (35.77%) studied up to primary level. But, at the middle school level, there is a sharp decrease in the proportion of girls as compared to the proportion of boys. This analysis of data shows that the parents allow their boys rather than girls to continue to study after their primary education. The survey conducted in Tirunelveli district exhibits a similar trend in the educational status of the sample population. However, the proportions of children from the different educational levels are not encouraging.

In both the districts, the parents of sample children believe that acquiring the skill of beedi making preferably at the age of nine or ten years would enable their children to earn more income and sustain their livelihood in future. To them, a child may not pick up the work easily if he or she starts rolling the beedis after the age of ten years. Especially in Tirunelveli district, the parents want their girl children to attend to the work at the age of six or seven years partly because they would save some money for their marriage. A similar view was held by the parents who send their girls to match factories situated in Kovilpatti Block in Thoothukudi district and Aruppukottai Block in Virudhunagar district of Tamilnadu.[4] Unlike these parents, their counterparts in Vellore district employ their boys and girls almost equally.

The amount of loan for pledging the children is based on their skill in beedi making. Again the target of either beedi rolling or closing beedi-end in a day is fixed depending on the amount of loan taken. On an average, daily earning of a girl is Rs. 11, whereas it is Rs.14 for a boy. They work for about 10 hours a day, from 8.00 am to 6.00 p.m., to earn this wage. But, what they actually get is half the wage or sometimes, less than this amount. The rest of it is compensated for the loan, i.e., taken as interest for the loan.

On the other hand, the act of pledging the children to the beedi contractors is not in vogue in Tirunelveli district because beedi making is done by the people in their domestic settings. Mostly the children join their mothers and other family members to do the work without wage. The target of work prescribed for the children in both the districts is more or less same. But the duration of work for these groups is not so. It is unusual to notice that the girl children in Vellore district sit with their mothers till mid-night to complete the prescribed target. On the contrary, their counterparts from Vellore are able to complete the prescribed number of beedis mostly in day time itself for the reason that they always work with other children in beedi units supervised by the agents meticulously. Therefore, they have to complete the target before the closing time of the units, normally after 6.00 p.m.

In addition to beedi making, the girl children in Vellore district have to attend to the domestic work of their employers. They have to carry drinking water from outside and look after the employers' tender children and sometimes render assistance in cooking and washing. The boys are sent to markets to buy vegetables and groceries. Thus, the employers make use of the pledged children for such domestic works without making any additional payment. The children do not oppose their masters as they are helpless and very much afraid of them. No doubt it is a typical form of exploitation under the guise of contract labour system.

This sort of exploitations forces that girls children to press their parents to shift them to other employers. A majority of children (about 50%) who changed their employers through their parents, report that they did so mainly because to get themselves relieved from their unkind and unscrupulous master who are always keen on exploiting them economically. In spite of their hard work, they are rather ill-treated by their masters in terms of scolding and physical punishment. Of the 500 pledged children, one-third of boys (33%) and the same proportion of girls complain of punishment by their present employers. Probably the rest of them do not want to reveal the matter to others as they are afraid of their employers. The information collected from various sources reveals that the agents and sub-contractors ill-treat the children even for petty matters. It is noticed that a long bamboo stick measuring 5'-6' was kept by the contractors for the purpose of beating the children without moving from their place in the beedi units.

Sometimes, the contractors would go to the children's residence to complain to their parents about their poor performance and misbehavior. In case the children are reluctant to come to the beedi units, the employers would to the extent of beating them, and dragging them to their units and making them work forcibly. Even if any child is still adamant, the contractor would tie one of his or her legs with an iron chain attached to a heavy iron or wooden piece. The data disclose that over 70 per cent of the parents felt that this sort of treatment confirms the employer's tendency of exploiting their children for personal gains.

The domestic child workers in Tirunelveli district are trained to go with the target-oriented work as their counterparts inVellore district trained by the agents of beedi units. Some time the parents seem to be ruthless in extracting work from their children even after late evening in order to complete the prescribed number of beedis to hand over them to the agents or contractors of beedi companies and collect their wage and raw materials. If they fail to do it within the specified time in a day, they will lose work for the day and have to wait till next to get their wage along with the raw material. Therefore, they compel their girls to go with a speed to complete the target without play and recreation. Most of them find it difficult to do so in spite of their continued work for hours together. This drudgery would cause a negative impact on them and some time drive few girls to the extent of committing suicide. It was informed during the field work in Tirunelveli district that two girls in 10-12 age group committed suicide owing to this reason.

There might be several household problems, but the parents in Vellore district need not go to the extent of pledging their children. In a similar way, the parents in Tirunelveli district should not be the exploiters of their own children by extracting work unscrupulously. If they desperately require the help of children in economic pursuits, they can as well make use of their service for a few hours both in the morning and in the evening within their households without affecting their studies. Nevertheless, these acts of parents violate the Human Rights ultimately by denying their children the right to education, play and the like during their childhood. The parents seem to be unmindful of their children's sufferings caused by this hazardous work. However, by and large, they want their children to support the family by their earnings. That is perhaps the reason why a majority of them started giving training to their children in *beedi* making before pledging them to the contractors or putting them to work in their homes themselves. In both the districts, nearly two-thirds of the children were trained at the age of six or seven to pick up *beedi* making. Nevertheless, the parents in Tirunelveli district are keen on training their girls in the work.

Generally, the parents in Vellore district relieve their daughters from the contractors at the age of twelve or thirteen years or immediately after attaining puberty by clearing off the loan in order to give them moral protection. If they have boys working in domestic setting, they normally put them to work in the place of their pledged girls. In case they are not able to repay the loan or have no sons to substitute their daughters, they have to continue the work in the *beedi* units. If it is not so, their daughters would be subject to sexual abuse or harassment in course of time. They would be treated humiliatingly by their employers if they are reluctant to move freely with them. This sort of incident does not seem to draw the attention of parents in a serious way. Consequently, in certain families, the working girls are indifferent to their parents.

It is found in both the districts that over 50 per cent of the fathers are alcoholics. At least two-thirds of them are addicted to it. Their families thrive on the earnings of their wives and children. They are more obsessed with liquor than family sentiments or loyalty. In such circumstances, the helpless mothers want their children to come to their help in maintaining their families. Therefore, they do not oppose their husband's act of pledging their children to the contractors. But, they feel guilty when they see their children coming home tired after a day long work. A series of Focus Group Interviews show that their concern for the children is more that of their husbands.

Except a few, almost all boys and girls from both the districts work for 10-12 hours a day. This indeed is too long for them to work. Almost all children report that they have heavy workload. It has been a painful task for them to sit to work by folding their legs for hours together. The long working hours lend them no time to have meaningful interaction with their parents and other children in their neighbourhood. These children ignore or rather sacrifice their education, play and other childhood activities for the sake of their families. In addition, they forgo recreation as they go home around 6.00 or 7.00 p.m. with no mood for recreation or play.

It is interesting to note that in Vellore Town, a considerable section of the children (41%) attend night schools maintained by the Indian Council of Child Welfare (ICCW). However, more girls (44%) than boys (38%) attend these schools. This would probably mean that the girls want to compensate their educational desire by attending such schools as most of them were denied education earlier. By and large, the teachers in-charge of the night schools at various centers, express that the girls are more regular and interested in pursing studies than the boys. This would, to a great extent, help them to get over the monotony of work.

Generally, in both the districts, the health condition of the children is rather in a poor state that their unsteady physical appearance would earn the sympathy of even a hard minded person. Their health problem varies from mild cough to acute tuberculosis. Nearly 50 per cent of them have respiratory diseases mainly because of their constant exposure to the tobacco dusts and *beedi leaves*. Since they are anemic due to malnutrition, they are highly susceptible to the respiratory infections resulting in frequent cold and cough. The condition of those who suffer from tuberculosis is more pitiable than the other children with some other complication. They not only run into the risk of becoming inactive but also pose danger of spreading the disease to other working children.

The *beedi* units in Vellore district are poorly ventilated. They are almost overcrowded with children, adult workers and materials. For instance, in a beedi unit measuring at a size of 15′ x 12′ nearly 20 persons are accommodated. On the whole, the work environment is not conducive to maintain normal health if not better health. In such a crowded and unhealthy atmosphere, the children are naturally subject to respiratory infections mostly by tobacco and beedi leaves.

Generally, the beedi workers lack personal hygiene. Since they are busily engaged in the work all the time in a day, they do not take bath regularly. The tight work schedule, ignorance and negligence of personal care together contribute to their lack of personal hygience. More or less one-third of the children in Vellore and Tirunelveli Towns inhabit in slums. These slums lack basic amenities conducive for living. There the housing and sanitary conditions are quite intolerable. Undoubtedly the slum atmosphere is also an important factor responsible for the lack of personal hygiene among them.

The policy of protecting the child workers from exploitation and improving their working condition will not solve the problem of child labour. The reason is that the protective measures prescribed by the Government would be undermined by the forces operating in demand and supply of child labour. Therefore, the most effective measure to eliminate the child work is perhaps the implementation of compulsory education stringently at least up to secondary level. In addition to this, various income and employment-generating schemes have to be introduced to enable the parents to run their families without either involving their children in economic pursuits or pledging them to the employers for a loan. Though it is long-term solution, it will check the problem of child labour to an appreciable extent. Yet another important measure in this regard is to create awareness among the people, especially the parents of working children.

Development Package

The District Administration in Vellore district developed a sound package in 1995 to counter the child labour all over the district. It formed a committee involving all key officials in the child labour eradication drive in seven sample villages surrounding the Vellore Town.[5] The first step was that this committee organised women of working children in a group in each sample village.

Each group was strongly motivated to practice saving habit. Consequently, every working woman started saving some amount of money according to their earning capacity. The required amount of loan was given to the needy mothers who in turn paid it to the contractors to free their children. But they had to clear off the loan by instalments over a period of time. Meanwhile the District Collector negotiated with the contractors to collect 50 per cent of the loan amount from the parents of the pledged children. Moreover, they were made give an undertaking that they do not provide loans to the parents who approach them to pledge their children. In a similar way, in village meetings presided over by the District Collector or any higher official, all women uniformly gave an assurance that they neither pledge their children nor do they allow their husbands to do so.

The children drawn from this work were given compulsory education in a non-formal way be qualified, unemployed, local and young graduates. In deed they expressed their happiness to get this opportunity of learning after a prolonged drudgery of beedi making. In order to generate family income, the mothers of working children were provided with milch cows and fodder with subsidy. It was proved to be a profitable business that boosted up their family income to an appreciable extent.

This programme went on well during the tenure of the District Collector who was instrumental for devising such an interesting package. Within a period of one year, the pledging system disappeared all over the district. Unfortunately his successors were not at it and as a result of this, it reemerged with all its paraphernalia. Even today it is in practice across the district turning several hundreds of children into pledged workers.

On the other hand, in Tirunelveli district, the population of child labour is in increasing trend. In spite of this, the District Administration is yet to evolve a comprehensive strategy to root out this problem. However, some non-Government Organisations are working to eradicate this menace by bringing back the children to schools after persuading the parents. The programmes relating to creating awareness among the parents and providing them or their adult family members with jobs for additional income would come in a long way to tackle the problem in the district. Moreover, the strict implementation of compulsory education at least up to secondary level would not only make the district a child-labour free one but also turn India a child-labour free nation.

The discussion in this paper is based on the findings of a research project on *Pledged Children in Beediworks in Vellore District of Tamilnadu* conducted in 1992 with the financial support of the Indian Council of Social Science Research, New Delhi and another research project on *Child Labour in Beedi Making in Tirunelveli District of Tamilnadu* conducted in 1995 with the financial support of the Union Ministry of Labour, Government of India.

The discussions in the paper relating to Pledged and non-pledged Children in Beediworks in Vellore and Tirunelveli Districts owe a lot to my articles entitled "Plight of Pledged Children in Beediworks", *Economic and Political Weekly,* Vol. 33, February 1998; "Health Risks in Beedi Making", *Social Welfare,* Vol. 44, June 1997; "Status of Primary-Middle School Education and Child Labour", *Journal of the Institute of Asian Studies,* Vol. 15, September 1997: and "Child Labour in Melapalayam", *Social Welfare,* Vol. 36, January-February, 1990.

NOTES

1. Beedi is a Locally Made Cigarettes Widely Used by the Labour Population.
2. S.W.P. Prabakaran, "Child Labour in Hotel Industry in Tirunelveli District of Tamil Nadu" (Unpublished Ph.D. Thesis, 2005).
3. Data Collected from the Labour Welfare Office, Tirunelveli (Tamil Nadu, India) in 2006.
4. G. Karunanithi, Assessment of the Status of Primary Education in Selected Blocks of Kamarajar and V.O. Chidambaranar District of Tamil Nadu (Project Submitted to the UNICEF, Chennai, in 1992), p. 25.
5. These villages surveyed in the first phase of the project were revisited to study the impact of the package developed by the district administration to combat child labour.

REFERENCES

Children and Women in India: A Situation Analysis, 1990 (New Delhi: UNICIF, 1991).

Vidyasagar, R. "Status of Children in Tamilnadu", in *Structural Adjustment Policy and the Child in India* (Madras: M.S. Swaminathan Research Foundation, 1992).

Karunanithi, G.Assessment of the Status of Primary Education in Selected Blocks of Virudhunagar and Thoothukudi Districts of Tamil Nadu (Project submitted to the UNICEF, Chennai, in 1992).

"Working Children: The Situation of the Girl Child", in *Child Labour Impact Assessment* (New Delhi: NORAD. 1994)

"Children Pay High Price for Cheap Labour" in *The Process of Nation* (New York: UNICIF House,1995).

Karunanithi, G. "Status of Primary-Middle School Education and Child Labour", *Journal of the Institute of Asian Studies* 15 (September, 1997): 127-134.

Karunanithi, G. "Plight of Pledged Children in Beediworks", *Economic and Political Weekly* 33 (February,1998): 450-452.

12

Plight of Women and Girl Children Engaged in *Beedi* Making

Projection of Some Cases from Tirunelveli District

Mr. L.T. Om Prakash*

Child labour has emerged as a serious global problem. It is a violation of child rights, which draws the attention of social scientists across the world. It is the result of the prevailing demand and supply factors. In addition to this, there is a great demand for children in the age group of 10-14, for jobs mostly in cottage type of unorganised sectors in rural as well as urban areas. It is mainly due to the reason that they are cheap labour in the sense that more work can be extracted from them for a meager wage. The parents are also ready to send their children for jobs in such sectors to earn for their family by sacrificing their education and childhood. The condition of girl children is comparatively more vulnerable than that of their male counterparts. In this basis, there are two major schools of thought regarding child labour, one supporting the regulation of

* **Research Associate, Centre for Study of Social Exclusion and Inclusive Policy, Manonmaniam Sundaranar University, Tirunelveli.**

child labour as it is viewed as the causes of poverty, and another supporting the prohibition of child labour, as it is the cause of exploitation.

On the other hand, it is quite observable that the trend of participation of women in this workforce is also consistently increasing over a period of time. According to the National Informatics Centre (NIC) sources, women constitute a significant part of the general workforce, especially a majority of them in urban areas primarily engaged in the unorganised sectors such as household industries, petty trades etc. Any way, the female work participation by status of employment indicates that there is a declining trend in the importance of self-employed category in both rural and urban areas and an overall increase in the casualization of the women workforce from 31.4 per cent in 1972-73 to 40.9 per cent in 1997 in rural India with a marginal decline to 39.6 per cent in 1999-2000.

Different societies have different approach towards children and women. For instance, the age thresholds for demarcating childhood and adulthood are also different. In some societies, age may not be a sufficient basis for defining 'childhood'. The fulfilment of certain social rites and traditional obligations may well be important requirements in defining 'adult' and 'child' status. International Labour Organisation (ILO) estimated that there were some 88 million working children between 10 and 14 years of age. According to the Factories Act, 1948, the Apprentice Act, 1951, and the Child Labour Prohibition Act, 1986, child is defined as a person up to 14 years. But according to the Juvenile Justice Act, 1986, juvenile is a person who has not attained the age of 16 in case of boy, and 18 in case of girl. The Child Labour (Prohibition and Regulation) Act is enforced on 1986, and is listed some industries, which should not employ children below the age of fourteen year. But, this law has nothing to do with children working as part of family labour. In case of women, they are subjugated to menfolk in many ways in the patriarchal societies in India.

One of the most exploiting unorganised sectors employing millions of children and women all over India is *beedi* industry.

Beedi is a local cigarette made of tobacco leaves. *Beedi* rolling is one of the major informal sector activities in the Tirunelveli district of Tamilnadu. At present it is estimated that more than 40 *beedi* companies are active in this part of the state. It is reported that *beedi* making is identified as a hazardous work. Children and women roll *beedis* mostly in unhygienic and polluting atmosphere, which are undoubtedly detrimental to their mental, physical, moral and social development. This research paper attempts to analyze various factors and circumstances that turn the girl children and women to be the victims in domestic as well as in factory settings.

This research was conducted among selected *beedi* making households from Tirunelveli district of Tamilnadu during September-October 2004. Case study method was used to collect data from these households. Observation method is also used to corroborate certain information. Based on the analysis of data, the researchers have found that the *beedi* making in Tirunelveli district is, in one way or another, a target-oriented work. For instance, the girl children and women engaged in this work are compelled to roll a prescribed number of *beedi* within a day. If they do not do so, they are subject to both oral as well as physical punishment. Sometimes, they are denied remuneration, which ultimately result in emotional imbalance among them.

Most of the girl children, after the implementation of Child Labour (Prohibition and Regulation) Act, 1986 do work at their homes because they are denied entrance into the factories. At the home, they are rather compelled by their parents, especially by their mother to roll *beedi* owing to poverty.

As *beedi* rolling is largely a home-based work, girl children and women are easily inducted into this practice. Thus *beedi* making has increased the number of working children and women in the unorganised sector in India. The conditions of girl children are lamentable, as they have to help their parents, especially, their mother in *beedi* making in addition to performing household chores. In some areas, skill in *beedi* rolling is considered as a special qualification for marriage and to pay comparatively less dowry. Women, who are unskilled in *beedi* making, are trained to roll *beedi* even after marriage, if the groom's residence is in an area where *beedi* rolling is the primary occupation. In some cases, girl children are compelled by their mother and other adult female workers to acquire the required skill in *beedi* rolling and to roll *beedis* to compensate the money needed for their marriage.

The condition of girl children is rather awful as they are subject to molestation and sexual harassment by some unkind agents/owners of *beedi* units. They are expected to be obedient to their master and follow their instructions without protest. If they are reluctant to yield to the favours of their master, they will be punished in terms of discarding several *beedis* from the bundles saying that they are defective *beedis*. It is thus evident that most of the victims of *beedi* making are girl children.

A working girl child expresses her problem as follows:

> I am thirteen years old, I turned to be dropped out while studying V standard. My teachers had positive opinion about my studies. I had keen interest in my studies. My teachers appreciated me several times for my handwriting. Now, I am using the same hands to roll *beedis*. I was forced by my parents to support them in *beedi* making during evening preferably after the school time. Eventually, I turned to be full time *beedi* roller owing to financial crisis in my family. As my parents are busy with *beedi* rolling and cow rearing, I have to do most of the household chores in addition to *beedi* rolling from dawn to dust.

Another heinous practice of parents is pledging their children to the owners/agents of *beedi* units. It is mostly prevalent in Vellore district of Tamilnadu during the past. These children are subject to harassment by the unscrupulous owners/agents of *beedi* units, if they are unable to keep pace with the prescribed target of a day. Hence, in several occasions, they are detained in the *beedi* units till 9.00 p.m. They are often subject to corporal punishment in order to complete the prescribed number of *beedis*. In Tirunelveli district also, the incidences of pledging the children to *beedi* owners and punishment given to them were reported in the past. However, the parents would punish their children, if they were not able to complete the target of a day. They compel their children to sit with them till mid-nights in order to roll the required number of *beedis* to handover them to the agents/owners in the next morning; otherwise they could not get the raw materials on the same day. Therefore, the workable device that they use to motivate and enable the children to complete the target within the specific time is providing the children with non-vegetarian food at least twice a week and money to go for movies at weekends in case of male children.

Dowry is also playing a vital role in making the condition of girl children worse. They are insisted to roll *beedis* to pay dowry. Teenage girls are encouraged to work interestingly by assuring them a handsome husband provided they must earn more money for dowry by rolling more *beedis*. Some girl children below the age of twelve will tend to roll more number of *beedis*. This is possible because they have acquired skill in this work. In several families, this is undoubtedly an essential qualification for them to get married.

The following statement provided by a girl child in the age group of 12, shows her plight:

> My family is confronting financial crisis. I have two younger brothers. I found that earning is better than learning. If I do not earn, my brothers will not get food. As I am earning regularly so as we get food thrice every day. In addition to this, I am also saving a little money for my marriage.

The condition of male children in *beedi* making is better than that of female children. But, it does not mean that it is tolerable. They are denied of food, recreation and education if they are reluctant to roll *beedis*. Most of the boys employed in *beedi* works are going schools. There parents feel that education for male children is more important than that for female children. Though, the male children are allowed to go to school, they are not assigned proper study time as they have to help their parents in making *beedis* after school time. Some boys are expected to fetch water, in addition to *beedi* making. However, boys are not compelled to take care of other household chores as girl children do.

It is observed that male children complain that they do not get adequate food. A boy says:

> I am rolling *beedis* every day after returning from school. My expectation of rolling *beedis* is to earn money to meet my basic requirements in life. My parents would give me two rupees every day after rolling *beedis* for three hours in the evening. I am making use of this money to buy eggs and other eatables available in the nearby shops. In the morning I am selling milk in the neighbouring areas. During holydays, I have to herd cattle. I rarely eat in the morning if there is no *kool*.

But, the nature of corporal punishment that has to suffer by male children is more brutal than that of female children. In many cases, male children, who go to play instead of rolling *beedis* in the evening are severely punished by their fathers.

In the following cases, a boy of fourteen years expressed his disgust about the punishment he received from his father.

> My friends asked me to play *kabbai* for my class in the evening. Though, I refused owing to the target of finishing prescribed number of *beedis* by the evening itself. But my friends made me play for my classmates to win the match. When I returned home, my father was ready with a hot iron rod to punish me. My mother cautioned me not to enter into home. As a result of this, I sacrificed my supper. Nevertheless, in the next morning, my father caught me and beaten by stick severely. Fortunately, I could escape from hot iron branding.

It is also noted that corporal punishment by teachers discourages the children to attend school and prefer other works. Some children have no interest to go to schools, as their teachers are very strict and punishing. Such children feel that rolling *beedis* is rather easier than undergoing punishment in schools. But these ignorant children do not know about the ill effects of this work. They are equally ignorant of the importance of education owing to adverse situation in family and unimpressive academic atmosphere in schools.

A girl of 12 years narrated his experience of *beedi* rolling as follows:

While studying V standard in a Government school, I was very poor in English and Mathematics. Though I worked hard to score pass marks in these subjects. I could not make it. So my English and Mathematics teachers punished me physically everyday. I developed fear to go school and reported to my parents about this. They had given me the option of going to school or helping them in *beedi* making. As I found *beedi* making was easier than undergoing punishments in the school. Hence, I started rolling *beedis*. Now my parents given me money at weekends for recreation and also buying eatables. The only problem is that I could not get time to play with my friends.

The following case shows how children are subjected to health hazards:

I am 13 years old girl. I am rolling *beedis* to help my parents financially. I start my work after morning ablutions and complete it in the late evening. Normally I roll *beedis* continuously for more than five hours in a single sitting. I do not feel fatigue if someone interacts with me while rolling *beedis*. Sometimes my younger brother in the age group of 10 would help me in the evening.

The following case expresses the plight of another child:

I am studying V standard, I am helping my mother in *beedi* making especially in the evening. When I was in IV standard, my mother promised me to buy a bicycle. Therefore, I was working hard to get it. Yet, I could not earn the required money to buy it. Very often, I feel bad about my school uniform because it is dirty and old. But, I do not want to go for a new set of uniform because of my priority to buy a bicycle as early as possible. I pray to god that the money saved for that purpose should not be spent for other urgent things.

The children are undergoing stress, as they have no time for recreation. Girl children are subject to punishment by their parents even after puberty. This would lead them in a state of emotional imbalance. Sometimes their mothers use obscene language to scold them. In many families, this is a common sight every day. Because, normally the mother would supervise their girl children during work at home. In the course of time, those children would undergo a psychological depression and develop antagonistic feeling against their mother. Most of the girl children reported that if they retaliate, they would become victims to the severe punishment.

Generally parents compel their children to roll *beedis* or persuade them to support them in *beedi* rolling. A mother says:

> I am 39 year old. I have three children: two girls and a boy. My husband is suffering from tuberculosis. He is unable to work hard. My son (aged 16) is studying X standard. I have no other option except to put my two girl children (aged 12 and 15) to *beedi* rolling. Now we are earning more than Rs. 70 a day. It is more or less satisfying our basic needs. However, I am unable to get medicine for my husband and also find it difficult to meet the educational requirements of my son.

Women *beedi* workers are also more prone to exploitation as most of those engaged in it are downtrodden and illiterates. Especially the *beedi* sub-contractors exploit them more severely. For instance, the women are provided with poor and inadequate quantity of raw materials by the contractors and summarily reject the *beedi* bundles prepared by the women showing its low quality and quantity. It adversely affect their earning and tend the adult female worker to pull her girl children into this practice to cope with the economic burden incurred by her. It is also observed that these women become the potential earner of the family as the male head of the family normally shed his responsibility of earning. They get shelter of the earning of their female companion. At the same time, using the patriarchal social setup, the male head assumes all power and privileges of the family head without contributing anything in return. In most of the cases, the male head of the family assume the authority of the earnings of the *beedi* rolling female head and their children. Thus, the irresponsibility of the father also contributes to the practice of girl child labour.

As such the girl children become victims to the exploitation of their parents and agents or contractors of *beedi* units. They are helpless due to family circumstances. This would affect their physical and mental development. The demand for child labour and women workers in unorganised sectors increases, as they are more obedient and sincere than that of adult male labourers.

Combating child labour is a prime area of concern for the development of human resources and through which the development of the country. Despite the constitutional provisions to promote the welfare of children, such inhuman practices still exist in one form of another. In addition to poverty alleviation measures, the implementation of compulsory education at least up to secondary level would also help the parents not to employ their children at their tender age, besides; the Government has to create alternate employment opportunities to the parents especially for the women workers.

13

Exploitation of Child Labour in Hotel Industry in Tirunelveli District of Tamilnadu

Dr. S.W.P. Prabakaran*

This study attempts to analyse the problems of child labour in big hotels in Tirunelveli district of Tamilnadu, India. Some of the objectives are: (i) to highlight the socio-demographic profile of the child labour in selected hotels; (ii) to examine their working conditions; (iii) to study their exploitation by the owners, cooks and supervisors. The study covers sample of 475 children drawn from all 95 big hotels situated in 9 taluk headquarters of Tirunelveli district of Tamilnadu. On the basis of simple random sampling, a sample of not less then five (more or less 50%) child labour were drawn for investigation from each hotel by tippets table. The data were collected mainly through interview schedule supplemented by observation and case–study.

Some of the major findings are that the majority of the children are from rural areas; all of them are from Most Backward, Backward and Scheduled Castes and none from upper forward castes; they overwork and are underpaid and illtreated. A great

* **Asst. Project Manager, A Poverty Reduction & Empowerment Project Govt. of Tamilnadu, Tirunelveli – 627 011.**

majority of them were punished by owners, where a majority of them were punished by Manager, Supervisor, Master and adult co-workers. Of the total, over one-third of them were pledged to the hotel owners by their parents for money. Of the total, over one-tenth of them were completed for homosexual activity. Thus, the hotel environment turns them into delinquents. A progressive nation like India must abolish child labour altogether.

Over decades India is increasingly facing the problem of child labour. Every third labourer in India is a child. Children continue to constitute an important source of cheap labour supply. Several thousands of children are put to work from dawn to dusk. They are deprived of their rights to study, play, health and the like. Consequently, by and large, they have lost their childhood.

It is reported that, in India, Tamilnadu State accounts for a large proportion of children employed in hotels, match works and fireworks industry, beedi industry and hosiery industry. All over India a considerable proportion of child labour is seen in all types of hotels. The parents and children mostly prefer hotel jobs, because the basic needs like food, shelter and dress are provided by the hotel owners besides wage. In addition to this, at any time, the parents can get an advance money by pledging their children.

A few empirical studies were conducted in the area of child labour in hotels, restaurants, dhabas and tea stalls in certain parts of India. However, they are not in-depth and elaborate studies. Hence by all means it is relevant at present to study the children employed in hotels. This study deals with child labour (up to the age of 14 years) working and staying in hotels located in certain urban centers in Tirunelveli district of Tamilnadu. This district was selected because of the reason that the proportion of workers engaged in various jobs is significantly high.

Objectives of the Study

In view of these observations, the following objectives have been formulated carefully:

1. To highlight the socio-demographic profile of the child labour in selected hotels.

2. To examine their working condition.
3. To study as to what extent they are exploited by the hotel owners, managers, and masters.

Methodology

For the study, out of about 1450 children, a sample of one-third (475) of children who are working and staying in hotels, were drawn from all 95 big hotels situated in 9 Taluk headquarters of Tirunelveli district in Tamilnadu. On the basis of a simple random sampling, a sample of not less than five (more or less 50%) child labour were drawn for investigation from each hotel by Tippets Table. The data were collected from the child workers, their parents, adult co-workers and hotel employers and employees by administering a well-constructed interview schedule. In addition to this, observation and case-study methods were also used to collect data.

In addition to the data collected from the child labour, hotel owners, masters, co-workers from the hotels, relevant information were also collected over a series of discussions with local N.G.Os, which are working for the eradication of child labour. The information regarding types of hotels and their sanitary conditions were collected from the Commercial Tax Office, Tirunelveli; Labour Welfare Office, Tirunelveli and Sanitary Inspector, Tirunelveli Corporation.

This study deals with child labour (up to the age of 14 years) working and staying in hotels located in some of the urban centres, in Tirunelveli district of Tamilnadu.

The study discloses that most of the children come to the hotel jobs around the age of eight. In Tirunelveli district, the number of hotels falling under the classification of Type I (boarding only) and Type III (lodging with canteen) is larger than number of Type II hotels (boarding and lodging). The study also shows that a majority of the children in the age group of 8-10 years (56%) join Type III hotels (lodging with canteen). After gaining some experience for an year or two, they shift to Type I hotels. Owing to better prospects like wage, security and food they normally prefer Type II hotels (boarding and lodging).

Therefore, a majority of the children in the age group of 12-14 years (62.9%) are found in Type II hotels (boarding and lodging) than in the other types.

The study also shows that a low majority of the children (69.4%) are employed in hotels located in tourist places. A considerable proportion of them (48.6%) work in hotels situated within the Tirunelveli Corporation limits. This is mainly due to the reason that these hotels provide more facilities, salary and tips than the hotels located in non-tourist places outside the corporation limits. Moreover, the children from the tourist centres secure hotel jobs relatively more easily.

It is found that a majority of the children (54%) have studied up to III Standard (semi-literates) and the rest (46%) up to V Standard (literates). The economic status of their families, due to their size and unemployment and or underemployment, does not allow them to be keen on education for these children. In Type III hotels (lodging with canteen), the proportion of semi-literates is higher than in type I (boarding only) and type II (boarding and lodging) hotels, because Type II hotels prefer children with at least education up to the primary level to facilitate easy communication with the customers.

The study shows that a great majority of the children (76%) are from rural areas. The main causes for their migration are poverty and non-availability of earning sources in their native places. Most of the rural parents prefer hotel jobs for their children for obvious reasons like the availability of accommodation facility, security and food. They send their children to towns and cities to secure jobs in hotels.

The study shows that a great majority of the children (89%) employed in all three types of hotels are Hindus. Very low proportions of Muslim and Christian children are employed in them. The Hindus form the majority among the population of the district. In the beginning, most of the Hindu children were engaged in agricultural operations. The failure of the monsoon coupled with a necessity of supplementing their family income forced them to work in hotels. Only a limited number of Christian children are found in hotels owing greatly to the efforts taken by the Christian Missionaries to educate the children by establishing a number of schools in Tirunelveli district. Only a limited number of Muslim children are found in hotels because a great majority of them are engaged in beedi making with their parents in their homes.

Nearly two-thirds of the children who approach hotel owners for jobs come from the Most Backward Castes and Backward Castes. The other third are from the Scheduled Castes. A negligible proportion (4.0%) belong to the Forward Castes. In Tirunelveli district, the parents from the Most Backward and Backward Castes do not mind their children doing menial jobs in hotels like cleaning the dining tables, washing the plates, tumblers, spoons and sweeping. But the parents from high castes do not want their children to do such jobs.

The study shows that nearly three-fourths of the children earn Rs. 500-1,000 per month. Their average monthly income works out to Rs. 685. This is a substantial contribution to their family income. The average monthly income of their families is Rs. 1,686 which includes the income of the children. The contribution of the children is 40 per cent. This clearly shows that the livelihood of the families partly depends on the earnings of the children.

It is found that nearly three-fourths of the children have shifted their jobs twice from one hotel to another hotel. The reason is that the hotels are not so lucrative to the children in all seasons. Besides they have to reckon with the problems caused by their masters, owners and adult co-workers. After some time, they want to switch over to other hotels. The children's tendency of shifting to other hotels is facilitated by the employment potential in the industry.

A great majority of children come from medium and large size families for hotel jobs. Large families supply more child workers than small families. The parents of large families expect their children to support them economically. According to them, more children in the families mean more hands to fetch an income.

An overwhelming majority of the children who are employed in Type I (boarding only) and Type III (lodging with canteen) hotels like their hotel job. This is mainly because Type I and Type III hotels provide them with food, shelter and security. Two-thirds of the children working in Type II hotels (boarding and lodging) like the job as against one-third who dislike them. This type of hotel also provides the children with similar facilities, but a considerable proportion of the children do not like the job because in these hotels the workload and working hours are relatively higher.

This Study deals with the working conditions of child labour in hotels. The working conditions of child labour include duration of work, workload, extra work and wages. The fieldwork for this project shows that the children are exploited at seven levels. They are: (i.) long duration of work; (ii) heavy workload; (iii) extra work, i.e., personal work of employers and employees, besides the assigned work in the hotel; (iv) low wage; (v) punishment; (vi) pledging of children; (vii) sexual abuse. The exploitation of child labour has been analyzed by correlating it with other related variables.

Concept of Exploitation

Generally the term "exploitation" is understood in two ways. It means, an extensive use of resources, natural or human. Secondly, a worker is said to be exploited if payment for work done is less than the value of that work. The latter meaning of exploitation was used by Karl Marx while explaining class conflict.

From the Marxian point of view, child labour is the product of capitalism and technologies it creates. Karl Marx considers the new technologies as an important factor that increases the demand for cheap, unskilled labour while decreasing the rate of profit that will lead the capitalists to exploitation of the labourers. Children according to Marx, are part of the "industrial reserve army".[1]

Children are undoubtedly cheaper and easily available workers as compared to adult workers. They are hired not only because of their readiness to be paid lower wages but also because of their possibility to this sort of exploitation. The employers are keen on employing children to extract more for long hours and to pay them less than the value of their labours. There are other reasons: (i) they are more flexible and they can be easily pressurized; (ii) they are trouble-free since they cannot organize agitations through unions; (iii) being minors, the membership of trade unions is not open to them; (iv) they do not demand over-time, medical and other facilities which the industry is supposed to provide; (v) employers find them more amenable to discipline, control; and (vi) they can be coaxed, admonished, pulled up and punished for default without jeopardizing relationship.

Forcing the children by their parents and pulling them up by their employers would easily turn them in to labourers mostly in unorganised sectors. In such industries, they are at a greater risk of contracting diseases as their immunity level is far lower than that of adults. Occupational hazards lead to a large number of accidents and more musculo-skeletal disorders among children as compared to their adult counterparts. A large number of these children are virtually confined to small rooms under inhuman environment and in most unhygienic surroundings. They are paid meager wages and are compelled to work in unsafe and unhealthy conditions. The hazardous conditions take their toll and they suffer mostly from respiratory problems.

A substantial portion of the workers are engaged in such unorganised sector. Their employment is characterized by job insecurity, irregular payments, and an absence of welfare measures. In India, children are exploited in large scale in the unorganised sectors such as un-incorporated enterprises and household industries (other than the organised ones) which are not regulated by any legislation and which do not maintain annual accounts or balance-sheets.

Besides economic exploitation, another form of exploitation obviously found the hotels is sexual abuse. They are often subject to this sort of exploitation by adult co-workers and other hotel employees. It is a common practice prevailing mostly in hotels with boarding and lodging facilities. Since, this study includes this type of hotels as samples, it attempts to explain this practice with the help of available data and case studies.

The main reason for this exploitation is that the adult co-workers have to accommodate the children in a common room exclusively meant for hotel employees. The adult workers take the advantage of physical proximity to tempt the children in to homosexual activities.

Another form of exploitation observed at the level of children is that they are pledged to the hotel owners by their parents for an advance sum of money. Like pledged children employed in cottage industries especially in beedi making in Tamilnadu, some children are pledged to the hotel owners at the time of employment by the parents entering in to a contract that the children should work in the hotels for a specific period compulsorily in order to compensate the advance. Therefore, the owners are keen on retaining the pledged children with the help of their managers and supervisors.

Long Duration of Work

In hotels, children normally work 12-14 hours a day. They are engaged in different types of work from early morning to late night. The number of hours of work depends upon a number of factors such as: (i) type of hotel; (ii) the situation of the hotel; (iii) the availability of child workers; (iv) the commands and orders of owners, masters and supervisors; and (v) the nature of work. Since no in-depth study on child labour in hotels has so far been undertaken in India, it is not possible to compare the findings of the present study with those of earlier ones. However, other studies on child labour in various sectors, mostly unorganised, have come to the conclusions that: (i) the working hours of children are long; (ii) adequate rest time is missing; and (iii) weekly and other holidays are not given. With a view to collecting factual information regarding the number of hours of work per day the child workers were interviewed. The information collected is presented in the following paragraph.

It is clear form the study that out of the 475 working children, over one-third (38.4%) worked 14 hours a day, and over one-fourth (28.4%) 13 hours a day. Almost one-third (32.8%) worked 12 hours a day. It is, thus, seen that normally the children in hotels work at least 12-14 hours a day. They start work at 5.30 a.m. and continue till 11.30. p.m. This shows that their working hours are relatively high as compared to the working hours of their counterparts in other sectors. But the Factory Act, 1948, and the Catering Establishment Act, 1958, stipulates eight hours of work a day for adult workers. The hotel owners compel the children to work for longer hours, which is legally an offence. They want to retain the children on the premises so that they could extract the maximum amount of work from them. They prefer employing rural children.

In Type III hotels, children work fewer hours than those in Types II and I hotels. The data disclose that two-thirds (65.6%) of them work up to 12 hours a day, one-fifth (20.0%) work up to 13 hours a day and less than 15 per cent (14.4%) work up to 14 hours a day. In Type III hotels, their work, which is mostly outside the dining chamber, is to serve the lodgers by supplying drinks including liquor, tiffin, meals and the like. On the other hand, in Types I and II hotels, more or less half the children work 14 hours a day. A majority of the children in Type II hotels work 14 hours a day. These hotels are busy most of the day. As the employers want to cater to the customers to the maximum extent possible, they extract more work from the children by assigning them various types of work for 12-14 hours a day. In a study on child labour in hotels, Sushila Srivastva and Bhanumathi concluded that over two-thirds of the children in the catering sector of Madras city work 10-12 hours a day.[2]

It is important to mention that the children working in hotels situated in tourist places work more hours than their counterparts in hotels located in non-tourist places.

The study shows that a majority of the children (50%) in hotels situated in tourist centres work 14 hours a day. More or less the same proportion (55%) of their counterparts in hotels located in non-tourist centres work 13 hours a day. In this context, it is relevant to refer to a study on child labour by Geeta Lal who finds that 38 per cent of the children work 9-12 hours in hotels in tourist centres.[3] It is obvious that the children from the former type of hotels work more hours than those who work in the latter type of hotels. Thus the children from the former type of hotels are subject to more exploitation than their counterparts in the latter type of hotels.

The time taken by the children to complete the work depends on their workload. They have to work several hours if they have a heavy workload. This is exhibited in the following paragraph.

Of 475 children, over one-third (41.2%) perform three types of work.* A majority (58.7%) perform more than three types of work.** Of the total children who do three types of work, nearly two-thirds (65.3%) work 12 hours a day. Of the total children who do more than three types of work, 60.5 per cent work 14 hours a day. Children attending to more than three types of work sweat for more hours than those who do three types of work. If there is an increase in the workload of children, they have to work longer hours.

It is already confirmed that the rural children have more workload than their urban counterparts. It is, therefore, a practice that the rural children work more hours than their urban counterparts.

The study show that out of 362 rural children, 44.7 per cent work 14 hours a day and out of 113 urban working children, a majority (53.0%) work for 12 hours a day. The reason is that the employers think that the rural children are strong and are able to withstand heavy workload. They do not hesitate to work for long duration and complete the assigned work. The employees think the urban children are not able to work hard and shoulder a heavy workload. If situations in a hotel warrant sharing a heavy workload, they run away and secure jobs in other hotels. These urbanites have gained experience in adapting themselves to the urban social environment.

But it is also possible that urban children are unwilling to work hard. However, it is clear that they do not protest positively against too heavy workload but run away to other hotels.

Note: * Upto three type of work:

(i) Sweeping and washing the floors and tables

(ii) Bringing in firewood and

(iii) Carrying water.

**More than three types of work:

(i) Sweeping and washing the floors and tables

(ii) Bringing in firewood

(iii) Carrying water

(iv) Supplying tea/coffee to the shopping centres.

It is also observed that employees discrimination between children introduced by the managers, supervisors and masters on the one hand and those introduced by brokers known to them directly or indirectly. The former category is given less workload. That is perhaps the reason why the children from the former category work for fewer hours than their counterparts in the latter category. If the employers or present employees are in one way or another responsible for recruiting the children of known parents, they show a concern for them while assigning them different types of work. On the other hand, they may not be so considerate to the children introduced by the brokers.

The study shows that of the total number of children introduced by hotel owners, managers, supervisors and masters, one-fourth (25%) have heavy workload working 14 hours a day. On the other hand, nearly a majority (48.7%) introduced by the brokers known to the hotel employers and employees have heavy workload, working 14 hours a day. It is inferred from this analysis that the heavy workload of children and long duration of their work depend upon the persons who introduce them to the hotel jobs.

Heavy Workload

When the children take jobs in hotels, the employers assign them one type of work either table cleaning or vessel cleaning or water supplying or room service or kitchen assistance. But after a week or a month, depending upon the types of hotel and their location, the children are assigned more types of work. The study explains the relationship between the heavy workload given the children and the types of hotel they work in.

The study shows that out of the 475 working children, 41.2 per cent do three types of work. But a majority of them (58.7%) do more than three types of work. Thus, the children are subject to exploitation in terms of extracting work making them work for more hours at a stretch.

In Type III hotels, over two-thirds (69.6%) do three types of work, and nearly one-third (30.4%) do more than three types of work. Normally the workload is relatively low in Type III hotels because the children are mostly engaged in catering to the needs of the lodging customers. The attached canteen is very small in size and prepares limited items of tiffin and food according to the requirements of the customers. The children carry such items and tea or coffee to the customers as and when they require. In addition to this, they supply them drinking water regularly. They also supply tea or coffee to the nearby commercial and shopping complexes between 11.00 a.m. and 12.30 and 3.00 and 6.00 p.m. But in Type I hotels, the workload is relatively heavier, because they are busy during business hours catering to the needs of the customers in terms of supplying varieties of tiffin and lunch from 6.00 a.m to 10.00 p.m. That is perhaps the reason why over one-third of the children (34.4%) do three types of work about two-thirds (65.5%) do more than three types of work. In Type II hotels, one-quarter (24.7%) do three types of work.

It is evident from study that out of 155 table cleaners, over one-third (37.4%) do three types of work, whereas nearly two-thirds (62.5%) do more than three types of work. Out of 127 water suppliers, 44.8 per cent do three types of work, whereas a majority (55.1%) do more than three types of work. Out of 110 tea suppliers, over one-third (36.3%) do three types of work, and nearly two-thirds (63.6%) do more than three types of work. Of 50 vessel cleaners, nearly one-third (30.0%) do three types of work, and over two-thirds (70.0%) do more than three types of work. Out of 33 kitchen assistants, a great majority (78.7%) do three types of work, and over one-fifth (21.2%) perform more than three types of work.

In hotels, the owners, managers, supervisors and masters assign one type of work to the children in the beginning and later they assign more work to them. A boy of 13 engaged in a hotel job in Tenkasi town describes his pathetic condition as follows:

> I get up at 5.30 a.m. and get ready for work at 6.00 a.m. Within 30 minutes, I have to brush my teeth, wash my face and smear sacred ash on my forehead neatly. Otherwise my master would scold me and sometimes beat me.
>
> Sometimes, I rest between 11.00 and 11.30 a.m. depending on the situation. By 11.30 a.m. I start cleaning the floor with liquid wash or mop and arrange the tables neatly. I continue

> to do the assigned work till 2.30 p.m. After that, I take food, which is kept separately in the kitchen. The time that I spend to complete my lunch (normally 20-30 minutes) is a simple matter, but it is a serious matter for my supervisor. After lunch time I clean the tables with acid and oil-soap.
>
> After that I have to get ready for the tiffin section after 3.00 p.m. and continue to work till 11.00 p.m. Sometimes, I relax for a while in the kitchen and sleep while standing or leaning against the wall. My supervisor gives me a slap to wake me up. He scolds me using filthy words. I normally do not take leave. The owner does not appoint substitutes for absentees. Therefore, the available workers have to share the work of the absentees. Sometimes, I have to go to buy vegetables, ration commodities and grocery for my masters. Before joining the hotel, I thought of only one type of work—either table cleaning or water supplying—but after some time, I have learnt to do all types of work.

This trend may perhaps be explained in terms of the difference between the rural and urban background of the children. The rural children are more obedient and afraid of the owners and other employers than their urban counterparts. They are more happier about the food they get thrice a day than their urban counterparts. Therefore, the hotel management assigns more work to the rural children than to the urban children.

This is perhaps the reason why the owners prefer rural children to those from urban areas. This is well supported by the views expressed by the owner of a hotel situated at Tirunelveli Junction. His views are presented as follows:

> I have thirty years of experience in hotel business. I have seen hundreds of children and clearly understand their behavior. I find that the rural children are more obedient, sincere, truthful and hard working than their urban counterparts are. Moreover, they do not often change the hotels in which they work. Unlike the urban children, they do not hesitate to attend to my personal and domestic work. They are more afraid of me than the urban children. That is the reason why I would like to employ more rural children than urban children.

The types of work assigned to the children are decided on the basis of the persons through whom they got the hotel job. It is a common practice in the hotels in Tirunelveli District as elsewhere that the managers, supervisors and masters recruit children of known parents. Sometimes they also take children of parents not known to them personally. They are more lenient to the children whose parents are known to them. They do not show such leniency to the children recruited through the brokers. This difference in the leniency shown by the middle management employees owes much to their personal relationship with the parents of the children.

The proportion of those who have secured hotel jobs through the middle management employees and who attend to more than three types of work is 40 per cent whereas the proportion of those who have joined the hotel jobs through brokers and who attend to more than three types of work is 72.3 per cent. It is thus evident that the children's personal relationship with the middle management employees plays a vital role in the allocation of work among the children. It is a common trend that most of the time the hotels located in tourist centres are crowded because of the increasing number of tourists every day during the season. This would result in an increase in the workload of the children. But it is not so in the hotels situated in non-tourist centers.

The study disclose that the proportion of children attending to more than three types of work in hotels situated in tourist centres is more than twice as much as the proportion of their counterparts with similar workload in hotels located in non-tourist places. It is evident that the children in the former type of hotels are subjected to more exploitation than those in the latter type of hotels. A 13-year-old boy whose duration of work is long in a hotel in a tourist centre explains his workload problem as follows:

> I work in a hotel located in a tourist place where there are three big waterfalls. In the hotel, the workload is heavy. There are 12 boys of my age doing different jobs. We start the work as early as 5.30 or 6.00 a.m. We complete the work after mid-night by 1.00 or 2.00 a.m. Our hotel is very popular in this

area and it has boarding and lodging facilities and also has a wine shop. From June to February this tourist place is busy because of the season. During this time hundreds of tourists from far off places throng this place. In order to attract the tourists, the employers and employees of our hotel extract more work from us to maintain it clean in all respects. They stand at the dining chamber most of the time and observe our activities closely. If we are slow, they scold and beat us.

When the hotels are crowded, the owner allows us group by group to have our tiffin and lunch within 15 minutes. We have to clean the tables and collect vessels as soon as the customers finish eating. Otherwise they shout at us and warn us using filthy language. Sometimes they mercilessly beat us.

We have to clean the floor three or four times a day and wash it with acid every night after business hours. Every day we have to bring the firewood and grocery items to the kitchen from the godown. At times, the supervisor changes our work. For instance, I would be assigned to cleaning and washing for two weeks and afterwards to assist the masters in the kitchen. After that I would be given the work of supplying coffee or tea to the customers staying in the hotel rooms. Sometimes, I would be sent to attend the customers in the bar. It is rather difficult to work as room boy because I have to walk up and down to fetch the items required by the customers. Though I get more tips, I feel pain in my legs.

Extra Work

In any industry exploitation of working children is observed in their workload, duration of work and wage. In hotels the children have to attend to the personal jobs of the owners, managers, supervisors, masters and adult co-workers. This is extra work for the children who are expected to do it without any return either in money or in kind. This is personal and domestic work of the employers and other employees.

The hotel owner has the power to recruit any new person or terminate his services. He provides the employees with food thrice a day and a monthly income. The manager, supervisor and masters supervise all sorts of work in the absence of the owner. Moreover they arrange the purchase of vegetables, grocery items and other raw materials, gas and firewood. Every month, the manager or supervisor calculates the income and expenditure of the hotel, distributes their wages to the employees and clears the income tax, electricity and telephone bills.

Since the children work at the mercy of the owners, manager and supervisor, they make use of the children for their personal work. In any hotel, there is one head cook who is otherwise known as master, assisted by four or five assistant cooks. The hotel owner gives importance to the master because the quality and taste of the food items lies in his efficiency and talent. He also makes use of the children for his personal work. Since the children are in need of tea or coffee at least every two hours to stimulate themselves to attend to their work and tasty food thrice a day they have to depend on the master. Therefore, he gets his personal work done by the children.

In addition to this, the adult co-workers have a hold over the children. It is a common practice in hotels that the children are divided into three or four groups. Each senior adult co-worker is assigned to supervise a group of children. Therefore, the children show due respect to the adult co-workers. The adult co-workers promptly exploit the children using them for their personal work.

Nevertheless, the first exploiter of the children in this way is the hotel owner. The work includes supplying him with coffee or tea, carrying hot water for him, buying cigarettes and *pan-parag* for him and the like. He sends the children to attend to his domestic work such as getting provisions from ration shop, collecting gas cylinder, buying vegetables and grocery items, carrying drinking water from outside and clothes to the launderer and fetching pressed dresses. In certain cases, the owners' family depends on hotel food. If it is so, in rotation, the children have to carry food for them thrice a day.

The second exploiter is the manager or the supervisor or the master. Most of them are away from their families because they are busy with hotel management. They take leave for a week once in six months. They live in houses close to the hotel. Since they live alone, they make use of the services of the children for their personal work. They send the children to buy things like cosmetics, *pan-parag*, liquor and cigarettes. They also ask them to clean the house and bring drinking water from outside if there is no tap connection.

The third exploiter is the adult co-worker who makes use of the services of the children to satisfy his personal needs. In this connection it is relevant to refer to the finding of Musafir Singh, V.D. Kaura and S.A. Khan in their study. They point out that most of the working children attend to the personal work of the owners like washing their dress, pressing their legs, massaging their body, polishing their shoes, etc. In many cases, they have to attend to the domestic chores of their employers.[4]

Though the children have access to their owners and other employees, they are more obligated to the former than to the latter. The owner is the superior authority. It is up to him to retain an employee or send him out. The employees have to live up to their expectations. That is perhaps why they attend to the domestic work of their owners besides their work in the hotel.

It is evident from the study that an overwhelming majority of the children (80.8%) attend to the domestic work of their owners. A majority (60.6%) do attend to the personal work of their managers, supervisors and masters. As they directly deal with the children, they have to oblige them. Otherwise, they deal with the children sternly and punish them unkindly. On the other hand, the adult co-workers move with the children in a friendly way. Therefore, the children prefer to be with them most of the time. The children confide their problems to them and seek their help and guidance. That is the reason why they are helpful to the co-workers.

> There is also a difference between the treatment of the children introduced by known persons [mostly the hotel employees] and of the children introduced by brokers who visit the hotels occasionally. The former group of children are taken care of by the employees because they secured the hotel jobs for them whereas the latter group of children have no guardians within the hotels. This leads to a variation in

the response of the children with regard to attending to the domestic as well as personal work of the hotel owners and other employees.

Low Income

The rate of payment depends upon various factors like the nature of the job and the skill acquired by the children. All the three types of hotels make monthly payment. Besides this payment, they provide the children with food and accommodation. The payment is made in three ways: (i) the parents collect the income of their children at the end of the month; (ii) the parents collect a small amount of money in advance at regular intervals instead of receiving the income of their children at the end of the month; (sometimes, the managers, supervisors and masters collect the advance money and send it to the parents of children); and (iii) the parents get an advance from the hotel owner (to the tune of Rs. 2,500-5,000) by pledging their children to them. This amount is decided according to the skill of the children.

There is a direct relationship between the duration of work and the income of the children.

It is evident from the study of 475 working children, over one-third (32.8%) work for 12 hours a day and earn up to Rs. 300 per month, and over one-fourth (28.4%) work for 13 hours a day and earn Rs. 300-600 per month. Over one-third (38.4%) work 14 hours a day and earn Rs. 600-900 per month.

Though the monthly income of the children increases with the increase in the duration of their work, their income is unjustifiably low considering the duration of their work. The hotel management makes them work for long hours and pays them very little. This shows that the hotel management exploits them economically. It is observed that there is a significant relationship between the location of the hotels in which the children are employed and their monthly income.

It is clear from study that the proportion of children employed in the hotels located in tourist places (73.9%) is considerably higher than those employed in the hotels situated in non-tourist places (65.5%) within their monthly income of Rs. 501-1000.

Since there is a great demand for workers in hotels in tourist places, the employers are prepared to pay them more than their counterparts in non-tourist places for the same duration of work. The children look for hotels paying more than what they get at present. That is perhaps why there is variation in the proportion of children from hotels located in tourist and non-tourist places with respect to their monthly income.

There is a significant difference between the income of the children and of their adult co-workers. It is observed that the suppliers who form the immediate higher category above the working children get Rs. 1800 per month from the hotels located in tourist places and Rs. 1500 from the hotels situated in non-tourist places for 10 hours of work a day. The children who toil for 14 hours a day get Rs. 600-900 per month. This is mainly due to the difference in age and experience between the two categories. Nevertheless, the children are assigned heavy workload and are subjected to physical punishment. Suppliers do not face such problems. In this context, it is relevant to refer to a finding of Musafir Singh, V.D. Kaura and S.A. Khan in their study. They point out that the children work for 12 to 16 hours in hotels in Mumbai, a popular tourist place, and get low wage. They feel that the hotel job is very heavy and continuous.[5]

It is noticed that the employers exploit the children by providing them with *beta*. For instance, if one or two children do not turn up at the work their work is allotted to other children. They have to attend to the allotted work besides their own work neatly and systematically. This results in a difficult situation in which the children have to shoulder heavy workload and assume more responsibilities. They are paid a *beta*, which, however, is rather low—around Rs.10 per day. For the meager sum of money, these children have to toil for hours together continuously. It is relevant to present here a case study.

> I am 13 years old and have been working in a hotel for 3 years. Many times the boys employed in the hotel do not turn up to work. Sometimes, one or two boys run away due to the physical punishment given to them. In such circumstances, I am asked to attend to the work of those

> absentees besides doing the work assigned to me. It is very painful for me to shoulder a heavy workload. If I do not, I will be forced. For that I am given a *beta* of Rs. 5-10 per day. Every time I experience severe pain in my hip, legs and shoulders. Sometimes, I am unable to sleep in the night due to this problem. I have decided to leave the hotel as early as possible. But I cannot leave immediately as my father has already received an advance of Rs. 2000 from the hotel owner. I have to serve at least 2-3 years.

Sometimes, the children are put to work at tea stalls within the hotel complex. Their main work is to supply tea or coffee to the neighbouring shopping centres at regular intervals. They are also compelled to supply at least an average of 100 cups of tea in the morning and the same number of cups of tea in the evening. This is understood from a case study.

> I have completed one year of service in this hotel. In the beginning I was cleaning the tables because the manager assigned that work to me. They then sent me to supply coffee and tea in the neighboring shopping centres. The supervisor asked me to supply 100 cups coffee or tea every day. This is a target fixed for every day. If do not complete the target, I will not be made permanent. If I continue to be so, I will be sent out after some time. After supplying coffee or tea, I have to collect the money regularly and hand it over to the manager in the evening. He is keen on observing whether the money tallies for 100 cups of coffee or tea. Sometimes, the customers may not be able to pay for want of change. If it is so, the total amount will not be correct, and I will be physically punished by the managers. If I am unable to collect the money from the customers, that amount will be deducted from my monthly income. Moreover, my income will be fixed based on the completion of my target and the correct settlement of account every day.

The discussion in this section clearly shows that the children attend to the assigned work for about 14 hours a day. However, in the course of time, they are assigned to do three or more than three types of work simultaneously. Thus, they are made to shoulder heavy workload within a short period after joining the hotels. In addition to this, they have to attend to personal and domestic work of the employers and employees. In spite to their heavy workload and extra work, they are not paid justifiably.

Punishment

In hotels, it is a common practice to find that the owners, supervisors, managers, masters and adult co-workers punish the working children if they do not perform their work as expected. They are scolded, or punished physically.

It is evident from study, a great majority of the children (83.3%) are punished by the owners, a majority (50.5%) are punished by the managers, supervisors and masters and 40% are punished by adult co-workers. It is thus clear that the owners punish the children more than the employees do.

In hotels, the punishment is of two types. One is oral and the other is physical. The data show that the types of punishment given to the children vary from person to person. This is presented below.

> In all types of hotels, nearly two-thirds of the owners and adult co-workers punish the children by scolding whereas one-third of them inflict corporal punishment. Since the owners are profit-oriented, they do not punish the children physically. They fear that the physical punishment would drive them out and as a result, they would have to recruit new children immediately in order to keep the work going. So they prefer to scold and try to correct them and retain them as far as possible. In a similar way, the adult co-workers punish them rarely because they are friendly and helpful to the children. On the contrary, nearly two-thirds of the managers and supervisors punish the children physically because they are keen on observing the performance of the children. When the children are lazy or slow in attending to the work and commit mistakes, the manager and supervisor punish them physically in order to correct them.

Out of 396 children punished by the owners, nearly two-thirds (62.8%) are punished orally. Over one-third (37.1%) are punished physically. Out of 240 children punished by managers, supervisors and masters, over one-third (34.5%) of the children are punished orally and nearly two-thirds (65.4%) are punished physically. Of 195 children punished by adult co-workers, about two-thirds (65.2%) are punished orally and over one-third (34.2%) are punished physically. Thus, the punishment given depends on the person who gives the punishment. In all types of hotel, most of the owners punish the children.

The managers and supervisors do not apply their minds to the question of why a particular boy does not do his job as they desire him to do it. They are only keen that for the moment the boy should be driven back to work. They seem to be confident that if one boy runs away, they would find others. They do not try to find the reasons for the boys running away with a view to solving the problems of the boys so that they would prefer to stay. Thus these middle order executives are not positive in their attitude even in their own interests. They seem to lack professional training. It may be suggested in this connection that professional training and at least a short exposure of these people to the theory of personnel management will do good all-round.

The managers and supervisors neither seriously look into the labour problem nor mind the children running away. When the children run away, the managers and supervisors promise the owners that they would bring some other children.

It is relevant to describe a few case studies which would very well explain the child abuse in the hotels. A boy of 14 engaged in a hotel job in the Junction area at Tirunelveli says:

> I studied up to IV Std. I have two brothers and two sisters. I joined this job at the age of 10 and I have three and a half years' experience. I have also worked in hotels at Mumbai, Thiruvananthapuram and Chennai. My supervisor here has beaten me twice with firewood.
>
> My master often asks me to bring firewood by tri-cycle. The firewood is stored at a distance of two furlongs from the hotel. Once after bringing firewood I was resting at the staircase. My master scolded me using filthy words and beat me on my legs with firewood. (Showed the scar on the legs). However, the owner met all the medical expenses to treat the wounds on my legs. After two months, I left the job.

> When I was working in a hotel at Chennai, I was asked to clean all the 24 tables continuously because most of the boys were on leave for a few days for Diwali. As I was the only person attending to table cleaning, I became very tired and sat on a stool in the kitchen for a while. When the supervisor saw me, he hit my legs with an iron rod (a big scar is visible). Then I was admitted in a hospital. The owner met all medical expenses. Afterwards, I left the hotel and came to Tirunelveli.

Another 12 year old boy doing similar work in a hotel at Tirunelveli Town explains his plight as follows:

> Once my master asked me to attend to his domestic work, but I did not want, to as his wife used to extract more work, sending me to ration shop, laundry shop, tailor-shop and market. I would not be given any tips for doing all this. So I did not want to go to his house. Angered the master poured hot tea dust on my right leg. I didn't expect this. I screamed in pain. (He showed his burnt leg). I had to rest for three days in the hotel itself. However, the owner met all expenses towards my medical treatment. But he did not permit me to rest longer than three days.

Chandragupt S. Sanon's study also describes the punishments given to children in hotels. According to him, it varies from scolding to beating in the presence of customers. The owners are keen on getting the profit, but they do not bother about the welfare of the working children. They know how to extract work from the children.[6]

The owners get the work done by scolding the younger children. If they punish them physically, the children may run away from the hotels, which in turn may affect the profit of the hotel. Hence the owners resort to oral punishment. The owners feel that when the children grow older, they become disobedient, insincere and slow. So they have to be punish them physically. The same philosophy is followed by the hotel employees. The level of exploitation of the older ones is higher.

Pledging

It is found in some hotels under study that the parents pledged their children to get an advance from the owners. This system seems to be an easy way for the parents to get money in order to meet their family needs. While pledging their children, they get Rs. 2,500 to Rs. 5,000. This advance is decided based on the skill of a child in hotel job. A sum of Rs. 5000 is fixed for a skilled child, whereas a sum of Rs. 2500 is given for a beginner. Though this advance may be helpful to meet certain needs of the family, it is at the cost of the children who are forced to sacrifice their childhood without education, play and other activities. This study shows that more than one-third of the children are pledged to the employers.

It is clear from study that out of 475 working children, over one-third (36.6%) are pledged by their parents for an advance and the rest of them (63.4%) are not pledged. They were introduced to hotel jobs by various persons.

The owners while offering the advance to the parents get their signatures on promissory notes or on stamped receipts. As a result of this, the children cannot leave the job or run away from the hotel. This is also a check on their part that they should not demand an increase in their wages. In this context, it is relevant to refer to a study on child labour by Chandragupt S. Sanon who finds that, in Allahabhad, some of the children became bonded workers in a hotel because their parents had received some money in advance from the employers.[7]

Normally, the parents receive an advance from the owners. The study shows that 70.7 per cent of the children's parents directly collect an advance from the owners and for the rest of the children (29.3%) their introducers (managers, supervisors and masters) collect the advance on behalf of their parents. Later the parents collect it from them.

The managers, supervisors and masters are fraudulent because they do not give the actual advance mentioned to the parents. This is brought to light while crosschecking the information collected from the hotel owners, managers, supervisors and parents. Nevertheless, it must be acknowledged that in this regard a few employers are honest.

Sometimes, outside agents also introduce children to hotel jobs. But they are not dependable and frank. It is reported that an agent had taken two children from a village in a neighboring district promising them he would secure hotel jobs for them. The children went with him. At last he brought them to Tirunelveli Junction to put them in a hotel. On that day, there was tight police security in that area because of communal clashes. The agent became restless because of the fear that the police may enquire about the children. In order to escape from the police, he left the children in front of a hotel and quit the place immediately. Since the children were seen crying, a policeman came to know of the episode. He handed over the children to *Saranalayam*, a home for street children, run by a local NGO. Later, this NGO was able to find the village of the children, identify their parents and hand them over to their parents.[8]

The practice of sending children to hotel jobs through agents or hotel employees seems to have been in existence for a long time in Tirunelveli district. And children are sent to far away places in this quest. G. Karunanithi has pointed out in his unpublished but recent project report that some parents in a Harijan Colony of Pudupatti village in Tirunelveli district sent their boys to Bangalore and Mumbai through known persons to get employment in hotels.[9]

A study by Walter Fernandes concludes that the agents and contractors who supply labour to small factories, hotels, and tea stalls and provide domestic helpers to private families, go round villages in order to recruit them. As the rural parents are very poor, they fall prey to the allurement of the middlemen. They send their children to cities hoping that their future would be better.[10]

It is obvious from the study that out of 174 pledged children, the parents of 43.6 per cent have got up to Rs. 2,500 whereas a majority of the parents (56.8%) have got Rs. 2500-5000.

Of the total pledged children, one-fifth (19.5%) have agreed to work for a year; over one-fourth (27.0%) for one and half years and a majority (53.4%) for two years.

A boy from Tenkasi town working in a hotel describes his pledged life as follows:

> I joined the hotel job at the age of 10 with the help of my cousin who happened to be a supplier in the same hotel. He took Rs. 3,500 from the hotel owner and gave it to my father. For that I have to work for one year. My salary is Rs. 300 per month. My work includes cleaning the tables and collecting the vessels. I do not feel unsafe in this hotel because seven persons (4 adults and 3 boys) from my native place are working here with me. However, I want to leave because of heavy workload and long duration of work. But I cannot do it, as I am a pledged worker here. Unless my father returns the advance, I will not be relieved from the job.

A father, who has pledged his son to a hotel owner, gives the following statement:

> I am a landless agricultural labourer. My wife is also an agricultural coolie. We have two sons and two daughters. The girls are engaged in beedi rolling. My sons work in a Hotel in Tirunelveli Town. My first son is 14 and the second son is 10. We belong to a Scheduled Caste. We couldn't meet our daily needs with a meager income. So I borrowed Rs. 5,000 from the hotel owner who belongs to a neighboring village, after pledging my first son to do cleaning job in his hotel. He is earning Rs. 300 per month. My second son is also a cleaner in another hotel and is earning Rs. 100 per month. I have taken an advance of Rs. 2000 for him. They will have to work in the hotel for a minimum period of 15 months. Every week I meet my sons and collect the money which they get as tips and *beta*. After one and a half years, I want to extend the agreement and will get a sum of Rs. 10,000 for my daughters' marriage.

It is distressing to note that about 37 per cent of the total number of sample children were pledged to the hotel owners. It is reported that there is no hesitation on the part of the parents to pledge their sons. This is the easy way for some parents to get money in thousands at times of crisis in their families. Primarily it is a violation of Child Rights for which the parents are not punished by the law.

It is understood that both the parents and employers are equally responsible for the pledging system in the hotels. It needs no explanation to conclude that the parents are the losers and the hotel owners are the beneficiaries who are keen on capitalizing on the opportunity.

Sexual Exploitation

In hotels the children are subjected to sexual exploitation. A minority is forced by the hotel employees and adult co-workers to yield to homosexual activity. In the initial stage, they resist such compulsion. But in course of time, for obvious reasons, they subject themselves to such activity because they have no courage to antagonize their manager or supervisor or master or adult co-workers.

Child Sexual Abuse

Child Sexual Abuse has been defined as any kind of physical or mental violation of a child with sexual intent, usually by a person who is in possession of trust or power vis-a-vis the child. Child Sexual Abuse is also defined as any sexual behaviour directed at a person under 16, without informed consent. However, there is no uniformly accepted definition of child abuse.

The perpetrator can be any one who exploits the child's vulnerability to gain sexual gratification. It can also include activities which do not involve direct touching. Sexual exploitation takes different forms such as:

- Child labourers and young domestic workers are frequently used for the sexual gratification of employers and other adults.
- Children are sexually abused within the family, Rape within a family has its own alarming numbers.
- With the advent of HIV/AIDS, there is an increased demand for younger child prostitutes.
- Children are used as attractions in sex tourism. Children are victims of a globally organised sex trade. In some countries this helps in bringing much-needed foreign exchange.

- Children are abused within the context of cultural or traditional practices such as Child-marriage.
- Children in institutions are vulnerable to sexual abuse from those who are supposed to take care of them.

Children in situations of conflicts, and displaced, migrant and refugee children are particularly vulnerable to all forms of sexual exploitation.[11]

It is found that 52 children (10.95%) have been approached by other employees for homosexual activity. Of them, the proportion of those who are approached by their masters (48.4%) is considerably higher than the proportion of those approached by the adult co-workers (36.5%) and supervisors (15.3 per cent). The reason is that the children mostly sleep with their masters (cooks) and adult co-workers in the same room. Moreover, the children have more respect for their masters than for their adult co-workers. Close to a majority of the children approached to engage in homosex were approached by their masters. Over one-third of the children are approached by the adult co-workers because the latter treat the former kindly. Often the former borrow pornographic and yellow books, hair-oil, soap, tooth paste from these elder workers and borrow money from them.

It is also found that of 52 children, 36 (69.2%) yielded to their masters, supervisors, and co-workers. However, a majority (58.33%) of them in Type II hotels (grade A), over-one third (36.11%) in Type I (grade B) hotels and 5.56 per cent in Type III hotels (grade B1), are used for homosex. Generally, they often remain silent about the abuse due to fear, guilt or shame.

Most of the hotel employees are away from their families and some of them are bachelors. Usually they sleep together in a common room. Many of them see blue films and read pornographic and yellow books. Many have sex with prostitutes, besides practising masturbation. These habits lead them to taking advantage of the chance for homosex with the innocent children who are more or less a captive group. Thus the children become victims to this practice.

In Tirunelveli District, especially in big hotels, there are 25-65 employees working. Most of them are away from their families. Quite a few of them are bachelors. Their recreation includes seeing films, playing cards, gossiping, loafing, and playing sex-related games. Some of the hotel employees collect cine-service sex albums and paste them on the walls and doors of common rooms in which they are staying. They also see blue films and read pornographic books. These activities tempt them sexually, but do not offer them guidance to live decently. Gradually this results in the kindling of their sexual urge. Consequently, they seek these children for homosex. Thus, homosexuality is slowly induced among the children. In turn, in their youth, they repeat what their predecessor practised.

During the fieldwork, the investigator had detailed discussions with five children working in hotels in Tirunelveli town. They reported that they had homosex with their master and supervisor. In this regard, it is relevant to present the statement of a 13-year-old boy in Tirunelveli town. He says:

> I joined this job with the help of my master. At present, I am cleaning tables and collecting plates. In the beginning, I worked as a kitchen assistant to my master. We slept in the kitchen or on the terrace. In the first instance, my master approached me for homosex during night time. I was a bit reluctant, but after sometime I started responding to his calls. Now both of us do it whenever we want to. He gives me Rs. 10-15 every month to see films. He treats me kindly. Sometimes, he is more affectionate to me than my parents are. Therefore, I want to be with him most of the time. However, I want to give up homosex because a friend of my age working with me is suffering from health problems due to homosex.

Another boy of 13 in a hotel situated in the Junction area of Tirunelveli explains his habits and how they have affected him.

> An assistant cook of 27 is very close to me. His wife divorced him. He has the habit of homosex. Initially he repeatedly approached me for oral sex in spite of my reluctance. After sometime, I started responding to his calls. In course of time, I developed a taste for it. Now I find it difficult to give it up.

> At one stage, I left the hotel and started attending to customers in public toilets and isolated places late in the night. I could manage to collect Rs. 10-15 from a customer. After some months, I could not get customers. Therefore, I was starving for sometime and slept in the bus stand and the railway station. Due to hunger, I sought the help of my hotel manager to join the same hotel. In fact, I had a tough time with him. He scolded and beat me for what I had done after leaving the hotel. However, I joined the hotel with great difficulty. Though I have given up homosex, sometimes I drink liquor as a relief from heavy workload and long duration of work.

A local Tamil eveninger published a news item on 24 February 2002 that children in hotels in Tirunelveli are forced by their masters into homosexual activity. A local NGO came to know about this and attempted to put an end to this practice with the help of the police. As a result of this, the NGO started a home to admit those children who had left hotels due to various atrocities done to them by the employees.[12]

Prakash Kothari has also pointed out in his study that some boys are employed in sleazy B and C grade hotels and lodging houses where, besides getting a hopelessly inadequate salary and leading a miserable life, they also face a sense of insecurity. In these circumstances, they are subjected to sexual abuse and sexual exploitation.[13]

The conventional thinking in India is that homosexuality is an evil practice and that it spoils the physical and mental health of the subjects. Homosexuality has not been either legally or socially accepted, as it is in many other countries especially in the west. So to a conventional person with social concerns, homosexuality is an evil in this situation. But one may leave aside the question of the legality of homosexual relationships—and the physical health side of the controversy, too—and yet see that the coercion in the matter can affect the mental health of the victims. The social stigma attached to the practice gives them a sense of sin and deviance, which may drive them into subterfuges and secrecy. This is a sociological problem in a society which is not permissive as most societies in the west and the developed world are.

The entire nation should take concerted efforts to tackle the problem if not in one stroke, at least in a phased manner. No civilized nation on earth can watch with unconcern the plight of millions of children toiling not only for their survival but also to sustain the livelihood of their families. It is paradoxical to note that India has made remarkable progress in science and technology, but has allowed this problem to grow to a monstrous size. It is the need of the hour to fight child labour with determination so that this social evil is rooted out once and for all.

REFERENCES

1. Joe Arimpoor, "Profile of the Child Worker"; *Social Action* Vol. 44, (July-September 1994): p. 63.
2. Sushila Srivastava and R. Bhanumathi, "Child Workers in Farrming, Domestic and Catering Sectors", *Social Welfare*, pp. 24-26.
3. Geeta Lal, "Child Labour in India—An Over view", *Social Change*, (September-December 1997): 3-4.
4. Musafir Singh, V.D. Kaura and S.A. Khan, *Working Children in Bombay—Study* (Delhi: National Institute of Public Co-operation and Child Development, 1980), p. 196.
5. Ibid.
6. Chandragupt S. Sanon, *Working Children: A Sociological Analysis*, (New Delhi: APH Publishing Corporation,1998), pp. 126-127.
7. Ibid.
8. *Nellaiyil Velai Vangi-t-taruvathaka Moondru Siruvarkal Kadathal*, Malai Murasu (19.03.2000), p. 1.
9. G. Karunanithi, *Report on Child Labour in Beedi Industry in Tirunelveli* Kattabomman District of Tamil Nadu, (New Delhi: Ministry of Labour, 1995), p. 106.
10. Walter Fernandes, "Child Labour and the Processes of Exploitation", *Indian Journal of Social Work*, (April 1992): 183.
11. *Convention on the Rights of Child*, India, First Periodic Report 2001, (New Delhi: Department of Women and Child Development, Ministry of Human Development, 2001), p. 391-392.
12. *Nellaiyel Sex Kodumaikku Alakum Siruvarkal, Malai Murasu* (24.02.2000), p. 4.
13. Prakash Kothari, "Sexual Exploitation of Working Children", as cited by Walter Fernandes, *Child Labour and the Process of Exploitation*, op.cit., p. 183.

14

Challenges Faced by Unorganised Child Workers

Dr. Shobana Nelasco*
Mr. A. Nilasco Arputharaj**

Abstract

Most of our children are less fortunate and are compelled to work in unhygienic and harmful conditions which are hazardous to their well being. These child workers, who are unorganised, are not able to be banned. Neither they are able to be brought under any category of organisation. This paper studies about the legal protection available for child workers in India. Then the reason for the demand for and supply of labour is analysed. After that the magnitude of child labour in India is studied. This paper studies the various areas of child employment. There are more than 52 million child workers in the world. Out of which 50 million child labourers belong to underdeveloped countries. India, Pakistan and Bangladesh account for the highest percentage of the child labour in the world. From a short study

---

* **M.A. D.C.A., M.Phil., Ph.D., Reader in Economics, Fatima College, Madurai-18. Tamilnadu, India.**

** **M.B.A., D.C.A., D.R.T.M., D.R.E., (Ph.D.), Doctoral Research Scholar in Management, Madurai Kamaraj University, Madurai.**

conducted in Madurai, it was found that these child workers are getting a meagre amount as their income. It is also clear that the child employers prefer children between 11 and 14. By sending children to work, we deprive them of their legitimate right of childhood. But there are some paradoxes, which remain unanswered are explained. Finally the cost incurred by the society and the child himself/herself are categorised under Physiological, biological, psychological, and sociological terms. To abolish child labourers laws and regulations should be backed by effective enforcement machinery.

Paper

Childhood is an interesting and unforgettable part in most of our life. It is a period free from all worries. This is the period when children need special attention, care, understanding, affection, love, educational opportunities and protection for their physiological, mental and social development in conditions of freedom and dignity.

But, unfortunately most of our children are less fortunate and are compelled to work in unhygienic and harmful conditions which are hazardous to their well-being.

Due to the complexity of the problem, we are not able to tackle the issue. Since child labour is an offence, we could not take any effort for organising them also.

In 2004 there were 218 million children working illegally[1] in the eyes of international treaties. Child labour is defined as an economic activity for children under 12 years, any work for those aged 12-14 sufficient hours per week to undermine their health or education, and all "hazardous work" which could threaten the health of children under 18.

This paper studies about the legal protection available for child workers in India. Then an analysis on the type of job, they are generally involved in are listed out. After that the magnitude of child labour in India is studied.Then the reason for the demand for and supply of labour is analysed. Then a short study was conducted in Madurai considering 50 child workers from five different areas of operation. Paradoxes that are difficult to be answered are also listed out. Finally the costs incurred by the child workers because of this social practice is also analysed.

Legal Protection

A small sample of 50 child workers was considered for a short survey, where their age, income and savings were analysed.

Finally, based on the survey and based on the earlier literatures, the cost incurred by the society and by the child because of the child labour is intensively studied.

In 1929, a commission was appointed to fix the minimum age of employment. Subsequently, the Child Labour Act, 1933 was passed prohibiting employment of children below 14 years of age. Subsequently, many more legislations fixed the minimum age for employment of children from 12 to 18 years depending upon the type of employment.

Article 24 of our Constitution says that, 'no child below the age of 14 years shall be employed'. Article 45 emphasise on free and compulsory education for all children up to 14 years.

Supreme Court in one of its verdicts says that all offending employers must pay a compensation of Rs. 29,000 for every child.

The formulation of a new National Child Labour Policy, the enactment of the Child Labour (Prohibition and Regulation) Act, 1986, the setting up of a Task Force on child labour, the adoption of the Convention on the Rights of the Child and so on have played their own roles against child workers.

The 1999 ILO Convention for the Elimination of the Worst Forms of Child Labour calls for the immediate elimination of all "worst forms" of work for children. The ILO aims to achieve this objective by 2016 with clear plans in place by 2008.

Areas of Child Employment

From time immemorial, child labour is in practice. Children shared the work of their parents and teachers.

There are four major categories of work the children are involved. They are: (1) Domestic non-monetary work;

(2) Non-domestic non-monetary work and agrarian work; (3) non-agrarian work; and (4) Bonded labour work.

Children are employed in agriculture plantations, forestry, fishing, construction works, brick layering, brassware industry, Auto garages, lock industry, Gem cutting industry, Beedi making, Tea shops and restaurants, pottery industry, Chalk industry, Slate industry, Bangle industry, Glass industry, Match factories, Fire works industry, digging operation, etc.

In our day to day life we come across children working as cleaners in restaurants, street hawkers, train hawkers, construction coolies, domestic workers, baby sitters, auto garages, shoe polishers, rags and waste collectors. Even many of us have small children at our house, to do household works and to look after our children.

The UN lists 12 countries in which an estimated total of 250,000 children are found in military service, amongst them Sri Lanka, Uganda, Nepal, and Philippines. The UN report lists parties in Burundi, Chad, Colombia, Côte d'Ivoire, the Democratic Republic of the Congo (DRC), Myanmar, Nepal, the Philippines, Somalia, Sri Lanka, Sudan and Uganda as recruiting or using children as armed combatants or committing other abuses and violations against them.[2]

Magnitude of Child Workers in India

There are more than 52 million child workers in the world. Out of which 50 million child labourers belong to underdeveloped countries. The International Labour Organisation in its report says, child labour forms 11 to 20 per cent of the workforce in the Third World countries. Out of the total child labour force Developed (industrialised) economies have *2.5 million child workers,* Transition economies have *2.4 million child workers,* Sub-Saharan Africa have *48 million child workers,* Asia and the Pacific *127.3 million,* Latin America and the Caribbean *17.4 million child workers,* Middle East & North Africa *13.4 million.*[3]

India, Pakistan and Bangladesh account for the highest percentage of the child labour in the world. A shocking distinct feature is that India is having the largest number of the world's child workers. According to the *Hindustaan Times* April 1989, the number of working children in our country was 44 million. That is 5.5 per cent of the total population. This child labour force constitute 68 per cent of the rural labour force and 24 per cent of the urban labour force.

Of the total population of 843.93 million in India (1991 census) 36 per cent or 304 million were below the age of 15 years. Child labour in India contributes 20 per cent of GNP and 8 per cent of workforce.

In India four-fifth of the total working children are employed in agriculture and allied activities. Andhra Pradesh is in top of the list with 19 lakhs child labourers. According to the report on child labour in industries, 1981 approximately 40,000 to 50,000 children below 15 years were working in Sivakasi and surrounding localities. Child labour is also prevalent in UK and USA. More than one million child labour from UK and more than 8 lakhs child labour from USA are in the list.

Supply and Demand

Poverty is the seed-bed of child labour. Poor parents send their children to work for reasons of economic expediency, the consequent denial of education setting in motion a mutually reinforcing cycle liable to pass down the generations. It is nevertheless less expressive to attribute the problem solely to poverty; schools are often prohibitively expensive, of poor quality or inaccessible. Cultural pressures can undermine perception of the long term value of education, especially for girl children.

The serious upcoming diseases have regenerated the supply side of the child labour equation. Households where adult members suffer prolonged periods of illness suffer dramatic cuts in income and forced sales of assets which are compensated by withdrawing children from school and sending them to work. Africa in particular has seen a dramatic rise in the new phenomenon of child-headed households, brought on by AIDS mortality. An estimated 10 per cent of all children orphaned by HIV/AIDS in Africa are heads of households, compelled to provide for siblings.

This supply of child labour is accommodated by the demand of employers for a cheap and flexible workforce, including small-scale enterprises whose owners exploit their own family members. It is a mistake to think of globalisation as a force for improvement in labour standards. Although large-scale manufacturing industries may not directly rely on child labour, backward linkages created through subcontracting labour-intensive segments of the product may be less compliant.

Girl children are in demand for domestic service, the invisible nature of which adds to their vulnerability to exploitation and abuse. Absence from official statistics is even more likely for those girls kept away from school in order to work for their own families in the home or on the land.

Poverty is widely considered the top reason why children work at inappropriate jobs for their ages. Other than this family expectations and traditions, abuse of the child, lack of good schools and day care, lack of other services, such as health care, public opinion that downplays the risk of early work for children, uncaring attitudes of employers, limited choices for women etc.

"The parents of child labourers are often unemployed or underemployed, desperate for secure employment and income. Yet it is their children - more powerless and paid less - who are offered the jobs. In other words, says UNICEF, children are employed because they are easier to exploit," according to the "Roots of Child Labor" in Unicef's 1997 State of the World's Children Report.

A Case Study in Madurai

This paper wanted to make a small case study of the child labourers in Madurai. 50 city workers were alone considered for study. 10 from Hotel, 10 from Automobile workshop, 10 from Vegetable Vending, 10 from Construction industry and 10 from Domestic work were selected.

While considering their income, 15 of them were getting below 300 rupees, 20 of them get 301-600, 11 of them are earning 601-900 rupees and only 4 were getting a maximum of 901-1200 rupees.

While studying the age, the group consists—two of them were 5-8 years old, four 9-10 years old, fourteen 11-12 years old, Eighteen of them were 13 years old and 12 of them were 14 years old.

Thus it is understood that these child workers are getting a meagre amount as their income. It is also clear that the child employers prefer children between 11 and 14 years of age.

Cost of Child Labourers

Sending children to work or employing them means, depriving them of their legitimate right of childhood. It may be temporarily beneficial to the family, but it costs heavily to the child and to the society. Following are the inferences derived from the case study and from earlier researches.

Physiological Cost

Tender physique and biology of children are vulnerable to the tasks performed by them. Their body is affected by injuries. Their bones are affected by skeletal deformities, fractures, dislocation of bones, disfigurement of body and etc. They are susceptible to diseases affecting nerves and skin cancers. Deafness and loss of vision may also occur. Sometimes death may also be the result.

Biological Costs

Unclean and unhealthy working conditions contaminated drinking water and polluted air cost immune competency. Viruses, Bacteria and Parasites easily enter in to tender and premature body and cause diseases like diarrhoea, typhoid, malaria, jaundice etc.

Cost of Hazardous Processes

In the world, 126 million of these children are engaged in hazardous work, such as mining or handling chemicals, which is otherwise described as the "worst forms of child labour". Children working in hazardous occupations exposed to toxic gases, vapours, fumes, dusts, smoke costing impairment of lungs, liver, kidney, respiratory systems, throat, ear, eyes and skin. By the time they reach adulthood, they suffer from chronic diseases like TB, asthma, bronchitis, anaemic condition and diseases of nerves. Noise pollution cause hearing impairment and psychological disorders. Working children develop lot of problems like body pain, respiratory diseases, burns and skin disorders, cataract eye, muscular and skeletal diseases, fractures etc.

Psychological Cost

Psychologically disturbed children may result in nightmare, ill-temper, lying and stealing habits. Consumption of alcohol and drugging, tobacco chewing, smoking are other ways to vent their feeling of inadequacy. Aggression, anti-social behaviour and delinquency are often the efforts taken to boost self-esteem. Working children become forerunners of serious psychiatric and social difficulties in their adult life.

Social Costs

Because of the child labour practice, their health, education and energy are sacrificed. It is also proved in studies, that the net lifetime earnings of a worker, who start working as a child labourer is much lower than a worker who join workforce as adult labour. Child labour aggravates the problem of adult unemployment.

Child labour also leads to anti-social activities. These children are used for smuggling, sale and distribution of liquor and poisonous drugs. Addicted children are also used as criminals.

Some solutions to the problem of Child Labour have been studied. Increasing family income could be a fine solution. But providing education that helps children learn skills that will help them earn a living would be a better solution. Social services can also be given to help children and families survive crises, such as disease, or loss of home and shelter etc.

Paradoxes of Child Labour

Few paradoxes are existing which makes the problem more complex and hence make it more difficult to be tackled.

Organised vs. Unorganised child labourers: These child workers are exploited to the core because they are unorganised. By organizing them, some solid efforts can be taken. But to help the children, can we make an illegal practice a legal?

Supporting vs. Opposing child labourers: Children are forced to be labourers because they are not able to get a single square meal per day. By banning child labourers, even that single time meal is denied. Is it justifiable?

Parental responsibility vs. Governmental responsibility: Everybody's responsibility becomes nobody's responsibility. Compulsory free education makes the Government an offender against child labour whereas the Child Labour Eradication Act makes the parents responsible.

Employer vs. Employee responsibility: Who should own the responsibility of abolishing this social evil—the employer who has employed the children or the child employee.

Conclusion

To abolish child labourers, so many efforts are taken, but unfortunately, nothing has brought the desired success. The foremost problem is that if these children are banned from employment, indirectly we deny their right to live. So we have to take efforts for the employment of their parents and for the children's education. When there is economic security, there will not be any problem for them to go to school. The schools also should take efforts to attract these children.

Further laws and regulations should be backed by effective enforcement machinery. Labour inspection and related services must be strengthened. Separate vigilance cell should be established.

The important effort that can be taken to eradicate this evil is by educating the parents regarding this evil, by assisting them economically and morally. Unless this problem is tackled at grass-root level, the researches, reports, seminars and workshops will not bear any fruit.

NOTES

1. www.icftu.org/displaydocument
2. "Child soldiers continue to be recruited and used around the world", says UN report *UN News Center* http://www.un.org/apps/news/story.asp?NewsID=20666&Cr=child&Cr1

3. Mike Dottridge, Liz Stuart , *End Child Exploitation*, UNICEF, http://www.unicef.org.uk/publications/pdf/ECECHILD2_A4.pdf

REFERENCES

1. Arup Maharatna "Children's Work Activities, Surplus Labour and Fertility" pp. 363-367, *Economic and Political Weekly* Feb. 15-21, 1997.
2. Gulhane R.S., *ILO and Child Labour*, Central Board of Workers Education (India).
3. Dr. Hajira Kumar, "Street Children—In Search of a Lost Childhood", *Social Welfare*, June 97, pp. 14-18.
4. *I.L.O., Targeting the Intolerable*, Published by ILO, Geneva, 1998. www.ilo.org.
5. Karunanithi.G, "Child Labour—Health Risk of Beedi Making" *Social Welfare*, June, 1997, pp. 9-11.
6. Mike Dottridge, Liz Stuart , *End Child Exploitation*, UNICEF, http://www.unicef.org.uk/publications/pdf/ECECHILD2_A4.pdf
7. Dr. Mittal L.N., "Child Labour - Ni end in Sight", *Social Welfare*, June, 1997.
8. Dr. Neethi Mahanti, "Gender Perspective in Child Labour", *Social Welfare*, April, 1997, pp. 9-12.
9. Dr. Patnam and A.R. Bhale Ras, "Child Labour—The Parents Perspective", *Social Welfare*, June, 1997, pp. 12-14.
10. Ram Ahuja, *Social Problems in India*.
11. Shantha Sinha, "Child Labour and Education Policy in India", *The Administrator*, Vol. XLI, July-September 1996, pp. 17-29.
12. Sevashree Mahapatra, "Stamps to Check Child Labour", *Yojana*, July, 1997, pp. 24-26.
13. Singh S.P., Child Labour—The Malady and the Remedy, *Yojana*, July 1997, pp. 21-23.
14. Sontakey D.R. and S.S. Pathak, *Combating Child Labour Practice*, Central Board of Workers Education (India).
15. Dr. Uma Joshi, "Restoring Childhood to Child Labour", *Social Welfare*, April, 1997, pp. 26-28.
16. Veena R. Sankanagoundar, "Child Labour, Hazardous and Harmful", *Social Welfare*, June, 1997, pp. 5-8.

Index

❑❑❑